Eryri / Snowdonia

40 favourite walks

The author and publisher have made every effort to ensure that the information in this publication is accurate, and accept no responsibility whatsoever for any loss, injury or inconvenience experienced by any person or persons whilst using this book.

published by
pocket mountains ltd
The Old Church, Annanside,
Moffat DG10 9HB

ISBN: 978-1-916739-03-1

Text and photography copyright © Tom Hutton 2024

The right of Tom Hutton to be identified as the Author of this work has been asserted by him in accordance with the Copyright, Designs and Patents Act 1988

A catalogue record for this book is available from the British Library

Contains Ordnance Survey data © Crown copyright and database 2024

All rights reserved. No part of this publication may be reproduced, stored in a retrieval system, or transmitted in any form or by any means, electronic or mechanical, including photocopying and recording, unless expressly permitted by Pocket Mountains Ltd.

Printed by J Thomson Colour Printers, Glasgow

Introduction

The dramatic mountains, lush green forests and remote coastlines of North Wales are home to some of the UK's finest walking. From gentle lakeside and riverside strolls to challenging airy hill walks and high mountain summits, and from hidden historic ruins to bold-as-brass castles and spectacularly-positioned forts, this is an area that has something for all walkers.

Eryri National Park covers most of the landmass here. With an area of 2132 sq km, it actually covers around a tenth of the whole of Wales. But there's still much to see and do outside of the park boundary and some quite wonderful walking too. This guide contains a mix of varied walks that showcase the best and most picturesque parts of the national park, as well as exploring the coastal areas that surround it.

The mountains are the biggest draw, with Yr Wyddfa (formerly known as Snowdon) attracting more than 600,000 ascents per year, giving it the quite credible claim of being the world's most climbed mountain. Numbers aside, it is magnificent – a shapely rocky pyramid that towers 1085m above sea level, casting long shadows over boulder-filled corries bejewelled with mountain tarns.

It is also, of course, the highest peak in Wales, and significantly taller than its English counterpart. This alone draws the visitors. Like most mountains, Yr Wyddfa doesn't stand alone, though, and whilst its massif reaches higher than the rest, it is just one of many mountain ranges in the park, all with worthwhile peaks to climb and captivating paths to walk.

Get away from Yr Wyddfa and you can also get away from the crowds (with just a few exceptions). Most of the countryside hereabouts feels lonely and remote, and it's possible in some areas to walk for miles without seeing another person. The solitude rewards the bold explorer, and you are seldom more than a few footsteps away from another breathtaking view or hidden gem.

Here, summits soar high above valleys carved deep into the rugged hillsides by retreating glaciers at the end of the last ice age, with jagged ridges providing drama while cairns and trig points represent hard-earned focal points. Lower down, quarries and mines offer an insight into a time when there would have been little peace to be had in these hills.

Beneath the peaks, forests cloak folded hillsides; their foliage hides tumbling rivers, many with rushing waterfalls, others watched over by the remnants of long-gone industry. These rivers race from source to sea, from mountain to mouth – there are very few lengthy watercourses in these parts. Where they reach their destination, there's more beauty to be found – broad expansive estuaries that rise and fall with the tides and provide a habitat for all types of flora and fauna.

The coastline is on the whole comprised of rugged imposing cliffs crashed upon by Irish Sea swells and broken only occasionally by sweeping swathes of sand or hidden coves. Mountains rise seemingly straight from the waves in places. These provide exceptional views and top-notch walking. Dotted irregularly along the shores are small but bustling seaside towns and villages that are well worth exploring in their own right.

North Wales is more than just its landscape, though. This is a unique part of the country, where you're more likely to hear the native tongue than English if you eavesdrop in the shops or pubs, and where reminders of the area's history appear around almost every corner in the small towns that dot the region.

Areas covered

For ease of use, this guide is divided into four areas. The first chapter, Heart of Eryri, is the area most visitors think of as Eryri, providing many of the walks in this volume – with routes venturing from lower-level forest forays, through rougher hill walks, to big days out on Yr Wyddfa, the highest peak in Wales. The second chapter, Around Betws-y-Coed, contains a selection of rambles in the northeast corner of the national park, including the Conwy Valley and some of its more notable tributaries. For the purposes of this guidebook, the penultimate chapter, Southern Eryri, covers an extensive area south of Beddgelert in which the walks are well spread out. These routes tend to be quieter than those in the north and east, but no less enthralling for that. The last chapter, Anglesey, the Llŷn Peninsula and the North Coast, features all the wonderful walks that fall outside of the national park boundaries. These are predominantly, but not exclusively, coastal walks and, while wholly different in character, are every bit as enjoyable as the others in this volume.

History

The majority of the area covered by this guide falls within the county of Gwynedd, which gets its name from an independent kingdom that once covered North Wales. Gwynedd was one of a handful of such kingdoms in Wales that were formed following the Roman withdrawal from Britain in 410AD.

The principality of Wales was formed in 1216 in Aberdyfi, just south of the area covered by this volume, by Llywelyn ap Iorwerth, sometimes known as Llywelyn the Great. It was recognised in the 1218 Treaty of Worcester by Henry III. A period of de facto independence followed, finally terminated by Edward I's conquests between 1277 and 1283, at which point Wales became an annexed territory.

Despite a 15th-century uprising led by Owain Glyndwr, still a national hero to the people, Wales became part of the Kingdom of Great Britain in 1707 and later,

Y Garn from the Rhyd Ddu path ▸

in 1801, part of the Kingdom of Great Britain and Ireland.

Wales's independent language and culture continued to hold sway, however, with a Welsh-language bible published in 1588 and, in the 18th century, the establishment of the Welsh Calvinistic Methodists, now known as the Presbyterian Church of Wales.

The 19th-century Industrial Revolution brought jobs and a surge in the Welsh population. The southwest was dominated by iron production and coalmining, and the north by the slate industry. By the late 19th century, more than 17,000 men were involved in slate production in North Wales, and Welsh slate was used on roofs around the world.

Industrial disputes and the First World War saw production slow and there are just a handful of quarries still producing slate in North Wales these days. The quarries and works left behind still litter many of the hillsides, though, and these provide some fascinating focal points on a number of the walks.

After the Second World War, Wales witnessed a gradual decline in mining and heavy industry, and the country voted on devolution in 1979 and 1997. The first referendum on self-government resulted in a large defeat for the devolution movement, but there was a narrow majority in the second vote.

The National Assembly for Wales was formed in 1999, and further devolved powers were apportioned to it in 2006. In May 2020, the devolved

government was renamed Senedd Cymru or the Welsh Parliament, and is now generally referred to as the Senedd. In North Wales today, agriculture and tourism are the main employers.

How to use this guide
The walks featured here provide a true cross-section of the area's best walking – from easy low-level walks (the shortest and easiest being less than 3km and pan flat) to moderate coastal, forest and mountain routes and longer more challenging outings that require greater fitness, more careful planning and the best part of a day to complete.

For all but the easiest walks, it is advisable to wear walking shoes or boots, and it is worth remembering just how fickle the North Wales weather can be, so carry or wear some waterproof clothing. For the longer, tougher mountain walks, it's also recommended that you carry a pack with food, water and spare layers. It is always worth saving these walks for better days where possible.

The sketch maps in this guide are designed to help you find your way by providing an overall feel for the route and where to start and finish, but for your safety and enjoyment it is well worth carrying the relevant Ordnance Survey map for the area, as listed in each walk description, and maybe taking the time to compare this to the sketch map in order to get a more detailed look at where you're heading and what to expect. For mountain walks, it goes without saying that this is essential.

All the walks featured follow Public Rights of Way or use paths that cross what is known as 'Access Land' or 'CROW Land' as deemed by The Countryside and Rights of Way Act 2000. This gives the public the right of access to land mapped as open country (mountain, moor, heath and down) or registered common land. Please enjoy the countryside responsibly and follow the Countryside Code.

Public transport
While every effort has been made to choose routes that can be reached by public transport, coverage can be patchy in remoter areas and some walks are only accessible by car.

Rail services are useful for accessing some routes in this guide. The North Wales Coast Railway runs between Chester and Holyhead, passing along the north coast. At Llandudno Junction, it links with the Conwy Valley Line, which calls at Betws-y-Coed and Dolwyddelan on its way to Blaenau Ffestiniog. Serving the west of Eryri, the Cambrian Railway's Coast Line makes it possible to access routes at Criccieth and Barmouth by train. In visitor season, the narrow-gauge Welsh Highland and Ffestiniog Railways can also be used to connect with three of the routes in this guide, via stations at Rhyd Ddu and Tan-y-Bwlch.

A greater number of the routes are accessible by local bus – it is important to check timetables before setting out – some services operate at weekends only or do not include Sundays, and they can change at short notice. Visit traveline.cymru for information.

The Sherpa'r Wyddfa bus service is a great option for avoiding overcrowded car parks around the base of Yr Wyddfa in the spring and summer season and links busier settlements such as Bangor, Caernarfon, Porthmadog, Llanberis, Betws-y-Coed and Beddgelert with walks from Capel Curig, Pen y Pass, Rhyd Ddu and Nant Gwynant.

Language

In most of the regions covered by this guide, Welsh is the first language spoken by the local people, and you will hear it wherever you go. You'll also notice that most signs are bilingual. It's worth knowing how to use and pronounce a few words, especially a few polite greetings and the place names you will come across, and this is easily achieved by following just a handful of rules.

Firstly, unlike English, Welsh is phonetic, meaning every letter in a word has a sound. The sounds of most of the letters are similar to the English pronunciation, but there are differences.

Sounds

C is always hard like the *c* in *cat*
Ch is like the *ch* in Scottish *loch*
Dd is like the *th* in *the*
F is like the *v* in *violin*
Ff is like the *F* in *off*
Ll is easy; just place your tongue as if you're going to say *lord* and then blow (*cl* as in *claret* can be used)
R is like the *r* in *red* but rolled
Rh place your tongue to say the *r* in *red* and then blow (*r* as in *robin* can be used)
W is like the *oo* in *zoo*

Try

Bore da (*Boh-re dah*) Good morning
Prynhawn da (*Prin-houn dah*) Good afternoon
Iechydd da (*Yeh-kid dah*) Cheers – literally Good health
Diolch (*dee-olk*) Thanks
Nos da (*Nos dah*) Good night

You'll often hear the word ***iawn*** (*yow-un*) used as a greeting (and many other things). This literally means 'very', so 'very good' would be ***da iawn***, but usually the ***da*** is left off, so 'good' or 'OK' becomes just ***iawn***.

Note: There are 29 letters in the Welsh alphabet with ch, dd, ff, ng, ll, ph and rh all acting as single letters and the letters k, q, x, and z all missing altogether. On top of this, w and y are vowels, making seven in Welsh against five in English.

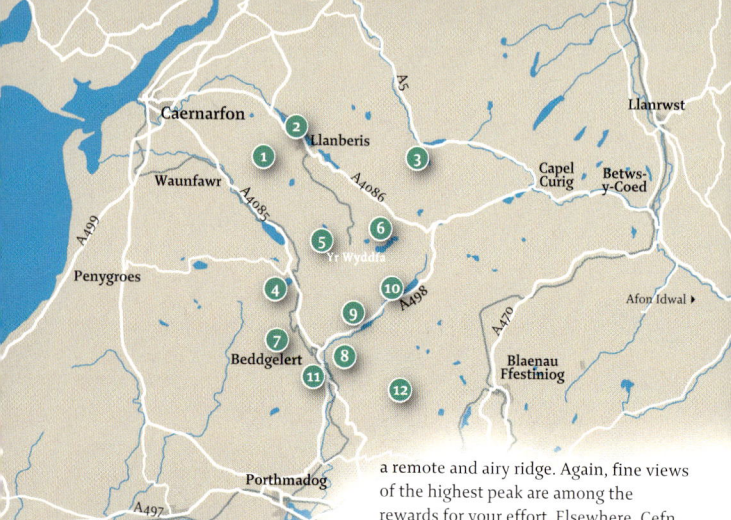

Yr Wyddfa is a beautiful mountain, especially if you choose to walk it outside of peak season and at a quiet time of day. This chapter features two of the most popular and attractive routes to the summit. However, there are plenty of other fine walks in the area, many of which give a taste of the mountains and the glorious scenery the area has to offer, without the crowds.

If you're seeking the high mountain experience, the ramble across Cnicht will more than meet expectations, and give you stunning views of Yr Wyddfa too. Another mountainous route in this chapter leads from the chocolate-box village of Beddgelert along the banks of the tumbling Afon Glaslyn, which rises up on Yr Wyddfa, before clambering up onto a remote and airy ridge. Again, fine views of the highest peak are among the rewards for your effort. Elsewhere, Cefn Du, the final outlier on Yr Wyddfa's northwest ridge, is explored in a blend of colourful heather moorland scattered with remnants of the area's slate quarrying past.

Eryri's lakes are as lovely as its mountains, and there are few bodies of water more breathtaking than Llyn Padarn, with its iconic views to the mountains and easy access to the village of Llanberis. Llyn Gwynant is also spectacularly positioned and sufficiently sheltered to often give a mirror-like reflection of the surrounding high peaks.

If you're looking for shelter, then three of the walks in this chapter stay mainly among forestry, making them perfect for bad weather days. The route from Beddgelert to Aberglaslyn is the easiest while walks from Craflwyn and Beddgelert Forest climb a little higher.

Heart of Eryri

1 **Cefn Du** 10
Make your way through old slate quarries to summit this little gem

2 **Llanberis and Llyn Padarn** 12
Take in some industrial heritage on this charming lakeside loop

3 **Cwm Idwal** 14
Enjoy a circuit of a glittering little lake surrounded by towering peaks

4 **Rhyd Ddu and Beddgelert Forest** 16
Hike to an idyllic lake hidden deep in the forest with views all the way

5 **Yr Wyddfa from Rhyd Ddu** 18
Pick a good day for this satisfying ascent from the lesser-walked south and west flanks

6 **Yr Wyddfa from Pen y Pass** 20
Revel in some spectacular mountain scenery on the shortest and easiest way to the top of the iconic peak

7 **Beddgelert Forest and Llyn Llywelyn** 22
Wander through beautiful woodland to reach an enchanting lake

8 **Cwm Bychan and Llyn Dinas** 24
Follow in the footsteps of miners on this high and remote circuit

9 **Craflwyn and Afon y Cwm** 26
Make time to appreciate the views on this steep but rewarding walk

10 **Llyn Gwynant** 28
Loop around one of Eryri's largest and most picturesque lakes

11 **The Aberglaslyn Gorge** 30
Explore a dramatic stretch of the glorious Afon Glaslyn from Beddgelert

12 **Croesor to Cnicht** 32
Scramble up the steep slopes of this Matterhorn-shaped peak which proudly overlooks the Glaslyn Valley

Cefn Du

Distance 3km **Time** 1 hour
Terrain a mix of slate walkways, narrow moorland paths and an occasional soft, boggy section **Map** OS Explorer OL17
Access Sherpa'r Wyddfa bus from Bangor and Beddgelert to Waunfawr, 3.5km from the start

From a distance, Cefn Du is no more than a scrubby, rounded moorland summit at the far end of Yr Wyddfa's lengthy northwest ridge. Up close, though, its steep heathery slopes are fascinating, with remnants of the area's intensive slate quarrying and sweeping views across the coast to Anglesey and the Llŷn Peninsula, as well as the high mountains of the national park.

Start at the small car park where the surfaced moorland road ends just short of the Bwlch-y-Groes slate quarry, about 3.5km east of the A4085 at Waunfawr (initially signed for Ceunant). Leave the car park, not by the main track that runs beneath it but instead by a faint track that leads to and then follows the fenceline above. Keep the fence to your left – this quickly establishes itself as an old slate tramway that makes a great walkway and carves an easy line through a sea of slate waste. It's worth stepping down off the path somewhere along the way just to admire the craftsmanship employed in building the embankment.

It now continues out onto a heathery slope – beautiful in late summer – and eventually merges with a broad track. Keep ahead on this and follow it through a gate onto the obvious double track leading to a prominent slate building, where you need to swing around to the left. Below, you have a fine view over

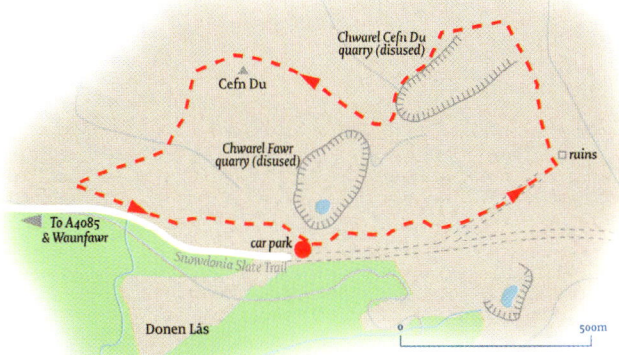

Llanberis and Llyn Padarn, and above these, dominating the skyline, is the shapely outline of Elidir Fawr, its western flanks a grid of quarried slate faces, separated by jumbles of waste.

Continue, now with a wall to your right. As the wall drops away, keep ahead on a grassy ramp beneath a slate stack to reach another gate. The next section gives some insight into the area's quarrying heritage as you weave through a confusion of buildings, levels and shafts, all the time working your way uphill around to the left. Pass to the right of some remarkably intact barracks before climbing steeply through a narrow cutting onto a grassy platform, dotted with ruined buildings.

You now have great views across a sea of heather to the summit of Cefn Du – the walk's high point. Bear left on the grassy path between buildings, with a shaft down to your left, and climb steeply up to the rim of the huge quarry. Keep the quarry to your left as the path leads easily around to a gate and an old slate stile.

Cross this and keep ahead. As the fences on both sides open out, keep right to climb steeply up with a wall on your right. This becomes a good path and leads through the heather to the trig point and summit – a magnificent viewpoint with Moel Eilio opposite and the summits of Garnedd Ugain and Yr Wyddfa beyond. The view in the other direction sweeps across Anglesey to Holyhead Mountain and the shapely peaks of Yr Eifl on the north side of the Llŷn Peninsula.

A path leads you from the trig point to a gate. At the gate, go left onto another path that soon drops with a fence to the right. At the bottom of the steep section, where the fence veers right, keep ahead to continue descending, now on a grassy path. This soon segues into a better path and breaks right to drop easily towards the end of the slate stack ahead. As you reach this, turn left to the very foot of the stack and then follow a clear path steeply to the top. A green walkway now leads back towards the start.

◀ Cefn Du summit plateau

Llanberis and Llyn Padarn

Distance 8km **Time** 2 hours 30
Terrain mainly good footpaths with a short section on a quiet road
Map OS Explorer OL17 **Access** Sherpa'r Wyddfa bus to Llanberis from Bangor, Caernarfon and Betws-y-Coed

The pastel-coloured town of Llanberis has become synonymous with outdoor sports. It is the traditional starting point for hundreds of thousands of pilgrimages to the nation's high point, Yr Wyddfa, and has also become a hub for the North Wales rock-climbing scene.

It wasn't always like this. Llanberis grew up around its slate quarrying industry and, although the last quarry closed its doors in the late 1960s, the scars – an incredible testament to human endeavour – are still clear to see on the steep slopes above the town. This walk passes beneath the quarries themselves and the doors of the one-time maintenance workshops which now house the National Slate Museum. It also passes the hospital and the mortuary. But it breaks free from industrial history too, looping around the shores of the town's beautiful lake, Llyn Padarn, and exploring some fine deciduous woodland.

Start at the Gilfach Ddu car park by the National Slate Museum in the Padarn Country Park (signed off the A4086). Look for the big white arrow at the far end of the car park indicating the start of the Lake Walk and follow the path around the side of Llyn Padarn to soon cross over the railway line which transported slate from here to the port of Y Felinheli on the Menai Strait, and on to Liverpool.

Continue up the wooden steps to the Quarry Hospital, which was built in 1840 to mitigate the impact of the high accident rate at the Dinorwig slate quarry

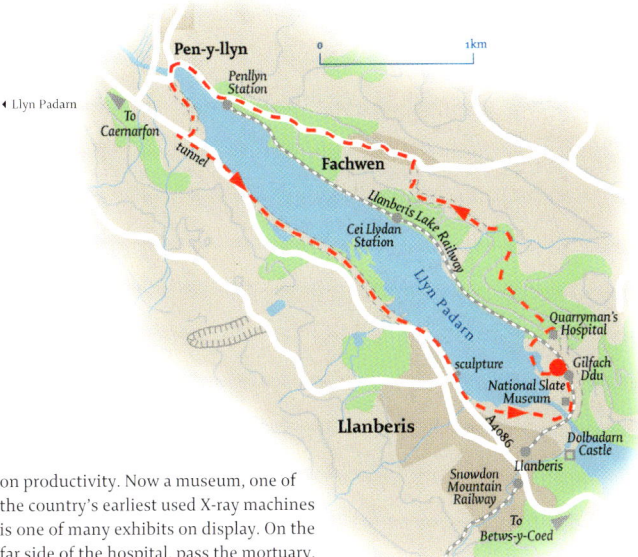

◂ Llyn Padarn

on productivity. Now a museum, one of the country's earliest used X-ray machines is one of many exhibits on display. On the far side of the hospital, pass the mortuary, where victims of fatal quarry accidents were brought, and head into woodland, with excellent views across the town to the Yr Wyddfa massif beyond.

Following the white posts, climb steeply, then descend to a fork and keep right to a gate. Cross the bridge over the Afon Fachwen to climb again, still keeping with the white posts and passing a quarry to eventually meet a road.

Turn left to follow this through Fachwen and continue down to the shores of Llyn Padarn. Turn left at a T-junction onto another road and cross the bridge at Pen-y-llyn – a fine viewpoint. Turn left again and follow this road to its end at a gate. Keep straight ahead to the main road and turn right, following the cycle sign for Llanberis, then cross and turn left through the old railway tunnel beneath the road. Continue ahead on the other side and now follow the cyclepath with Llyn Padarn on your left. Look out for the towering steel sword sculpture by the lakeside which honours the Princes of Gwynedd as you pass the car parks.

At the southwestern tip of the lake, a grassy trail leads across the Cae'r Ddol meadows to a footbridge which crosses the Afon y Bala with the ruined high round tower of Dolbadarn Castle off to the right at the head of Llyn Peris. Cross over the footbridge and turn left past the National Slate Museum to the car park at the start.

Cwm Idwal

Distance 4km **Time** 1 hour 30
Terrain good footpaths **Map** OS Explorer
OL17 **Access** bus to Ogwen Cottage from
Betws-y-Coed and Bangor

Resembling a glittering gem set in a rugged surround of towering grey rock, the blue-green waters of Llyn Idwal lie at the heart of some of the finest mountain scenery in the country. According to legend, the lake is named after the son of the 12th-century prince Owain Gwynedd who was drowned here by his jealous uncle Nefydd. It is also said that birds who live here have kept a vow, made in memory of the unfortunate prince, not to fly over the water where he perished.

The towering peaks of Glyder Fawr and Y Garn cast huge shadows over the crystal waters, and jagged ridges punctuate the scene, climbing steeply from the shores to the summits. The cirque that surrounds the lake is a National Nature Reserve, valued for its arctic-alpine flora, remnants from the last great ice age, maintaining a tenuous grip at the most southerly point of their range. Look also for mountain birds like the meadow pipit, the skylark and even the ringed ouzel, or mountain blackbird as it's often known.

Start at the Canolfan Cwm Idwal visitor centre, located by the A5, about 8km south of Bethesda and 6.5km west of Capel Curig, at Llyn Ogwen's western end. From the car park next to Idwal Cottage YHA, pick up the stepped path that leads

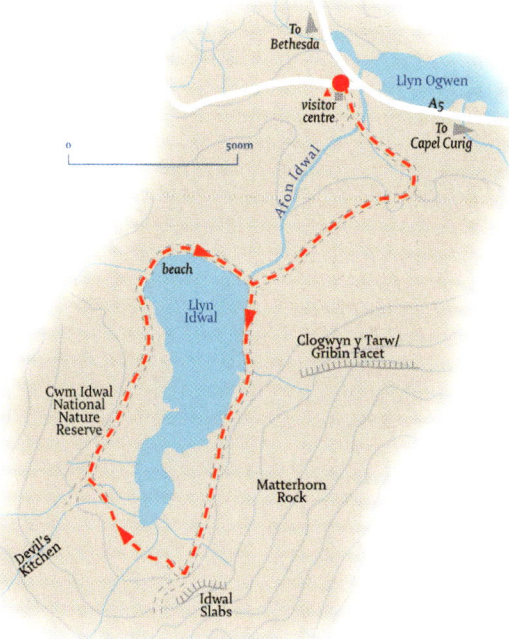

away from the visitor centre and ignore a branch off to the right to follow the main track around to the left, over a bridge. Now follow this track around to the right and easily upwards to the shores of Llyn Idwal. Keep left at the lake and continue on the main path with the water to your right. Follow the shore easily along, through a gate, and then continue towards the foot of the steep grey slabs clearly visible ahead. Known as the Idwal Slabs, these are very popular with rock climbers. Charles Darwin also visited here in 1831, and again 10 years later, when investigating theories around glaciation.

At the slabs, turn right down a stepped ramp and follow the now level path around the head of Llyn Idwal. At the far side, as the ground starts to steepen again, you join another path – this one drops from the Devil's Kitchen (a deep cleft in the rock up to your left). Turn right onto this path and follow it along the lake shore again, finally passing through a gate which gives access to a lovely beach.

Enjoy the views before continuing around to meet your outward path. Now all you need to do is retrace your earlier footsteps back to the car park.

◀ Llyn Idwal

Rhyd Ddu and Beddgelert Forest

Distance 9km **Time** 3 hours
Terrain a clear but often muddy path across sheep pasture and well-surfaced forest tracks **Map** OS Explorer OL17
Access Sherpa'r Wyddfa bus to Rhyd Ddu from Beddgelert, Bangor and Caernarfon

The lovely Llyn Llywelyn, cradled deep inside Beddgelert Forest, is the objective of this moderate walk which for the most part crosses open ground with incredible views over the Yr Wyddfa range, the Nantlle Ridge and Moel Hebog.

The opening leg climbs high above the valley, crossing rough sheep pasture, all the time with the imposing slopes of Y Garn towering overhead. It eventually levels and crosses a tumbling mountain stream before diving headfirst into the upper reaches of the forest. Forest roads then lead easily to Llyn Llywelyn, making a full lap of the shimmering waters – all the time in the shadow of the mighty Moel Hebog. More forest tracks lead away from the lake and onto Lôn Gwyrfai – a well-surfaced multi-use path that links Beddgelert village with Rhyd Ddu, eventually continuing towards Caernarfon. This is a wonderful section of the walk, at one stage passing close to another lake, Llyn y Gader, this one lined with majestic Caledonian pines.

From the Rhyd Ddu car park next to the bus stop and railway station on the A4085, cross the road and go through the gate and up a path. Turn right at the junction to continue out towards the road, then turn left through another gate to walk directly towards the towering peak of Y Garn. Continue through gates and up to a fork, where you keep left – the right-hand path heads straight up onto Y Garn. Go around the hillside, dropping to cross a small stream and then eventually crossing another, this one with waterfalls above and below.

Rhyd Ddu and Beddgelert Forest

tables on a small peninsula. Enjoy the views over the lake, and perhaps a seat and some lunch, before proceeding.

Head back onto the path and continue to a junction with a forest track. Turn right to follow this down for a few paces to a crossroads. Turn left here and enjoy easy walking to another crossroads, this one with a rough track to the left and a broad forest track to the right. Keep straight ahead here, and then ignore a turning on the right and another on the left, to continue to the next left, which is waymarked for Rhyd Ddu.

Follow this, keeping right at a fork, and you'll eventually emerge onto open ground. Keep ahead, now with Llyn y Gader down to your right. There are some great places to stop and enjoy the views if you have time. Continue over a footbridge and into some quarry ruins, where a gate gives access to an old level, which is now a footpath. Turn right onto this and enjoy easy walking with fine views as you pass the west shore of the lake. You'll eventually reach a junction with your outward path. Turn right here and follow it back to the car park.

Carry on into the forest and at the main forest track, cross to keep straight ahead on a small path that leads between boulders. This emerges on another forest track, where you keep straight ahead again. At the next junction, turn sharp left and then ignore a rough track to the left to continue to another fork, where you go left. Stay with this now, ignoring a final turn on the left after 1km, and now loop all the way around Llyn Llywelyn. On the far side, you'll see a clear path leading left, along the dam. Take this to the picnic

Yr Wyddfa from Rhyd Ddu

Distance 15km Time 6 hours
Terrain rough footpaths, some steep ground and exposure; 3km on the A4085 to finish (bus alternative)
Map OS Explorer OL17 Access Sherpa'r Wyddfa bus to Rhyd Ddu from Beddgelert, Bangor and Caernarfon

The south and west flanks of Yr Wyddfa are notably quieter than the other side but still offer fine walks to the summit. This walk starts at Rhyd Ddu and climbs easily at first onto the mountain's south ridge, where it gets a little more challenging before reaching the top.

Start at the north end of the car park adjacent to Rhyd Ddu Station. Keeping the toilet block to your left, follow signs to Yr Wyddfa along a tarmac track. After a short distance, cross the railway track via metal gates to join a good stony track. Follow this easily up, shortly bearing right around a barrier where a farm drive leads left.

Continue through quarry remains and pass a farm shed to your left. Carry on uphill, staying on the broad stony track to go through a gate. A short while after passing through another gate, you'll come to a fork, with the Rhyd Ddu Path signed left. Follow this through a gate to join a much rougher, narrower path which soon gives views up towards the summit.

Wind through rocky outcrops and pass through a couple of gates where it starts to get steeper. Another gate leads onto the clifftops of Llechog, where you have spectacular views down over the twin lakes of Llyn Coch and Llyn Nadroedd.

Continue upwards, zigzagging the final stretch, then keeping left at a junction to traverse to a notch in the south ridge

Yr Wyddfa from Rhyd Ddu

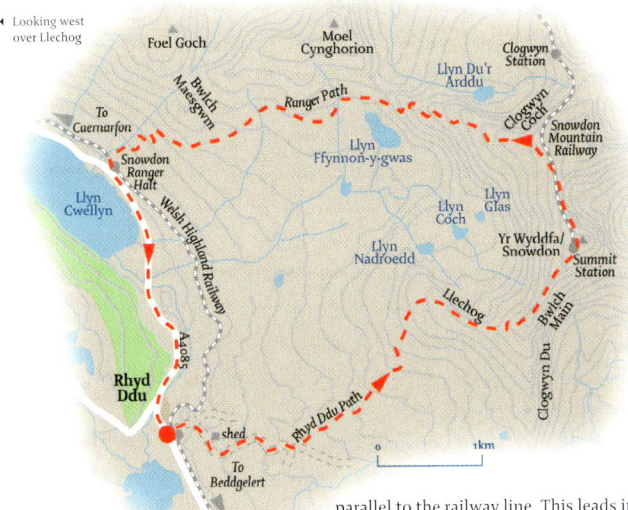

◀ Looking west over Llechog

known as Bwlch Main. This is a stunning spot, with great views south over Cwm Llan and the elegant peak of Y Lliwedd above it. Continuing, the rough path up the south ridge is exposed in places and hands may be needed at times. This terminates on steps that lead to Hafod Eryri – the summit visitor centre and café. The summit itself is every bit as good a viewpoint as you'd expect for the highest mountain in Wales.

For a satisfying circular route, it's best now to descend the Ranger Path, but this does mean a bus ride or a 3km walk on the road to finish. If you'd rather not, it's easy to retrace your ascent. Otherwise, with Hafod Eryri to your left, walk down steps from the summit and follow a rough path, parallel to the railway line. This leads into a broad saddle, marked with a standing stone. Fork left here, cross the railway, then follow the clear path across the hillside. This then trends leftwards and descends more steeply, eventually in a series of switchbacks. Where the gradient relents, keep straight ahead to a gate. The path now leads easily across the hillside, through further gates and past a major junction, where a path leads right to Bwlch Maesgwm.

Carry on ahead with views down over Llyn Cwellyn and the Nantlle Ridge on the far side of the valley. Further gates lead onto a series of zigzags that take you down past a farmhouse to the road at Snowdon Ranger. Turn left here to follow the road, or you can catch the bus back to Rhyd Ddu.

Yr Wyddfa from Pen y Pass

Distance 12km **Time** 5 hours
Terrain footpaths which are rough in places, some steep ground and exposure
Map OS Explorer OL17 **Access** Sherpa'r Wyddfa bus to Pen y Pass from Betws-y-Coed, Caernarfon and Llanberis

This is the shortest and easiest route to Yr Wyddf's summit. It's also incredibly spectacular – climbing through the atmospheric Bwlch y Moch and beneath the jagged peak of Crib Goch, then traversing the hillside high up and deep in the mountain's eastern cwm.

The final clamber up to Bwlch Glas is steep and strenuous and it really feels like you're climbing a big mountain. The descent is also steep as far as the shores of Llyn Llydaw, but after that it's an easy stroll out on a good track. Parking at Pen y Pass can be difficult and needs pre-booking, but there are also buses from the Llanberis Pass and Nant Peris.

The Pen y Pass car park is located on the A4086, 9km southeast of Llanberis. Head out of the top right-hand corner of the car park – clearly signed as the Pyg Track – and simply follow the steep, rough, undulating path around the hillside with great views down over the Llanberis Pass and up towards the summit of Crib Goch. Continue like this for some time and

Yr Wyddfa from Pen y Pass

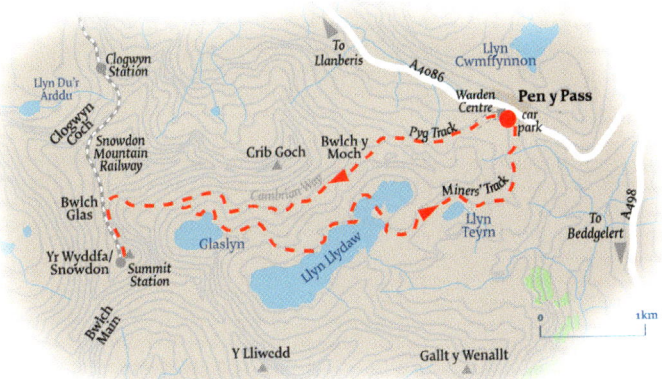

you'll eventually meet a drystone wall that leads into Bwlch y Moch.

Follow the sign ahead to cross a double stile on the main path. The next section traverses the hillside with amazing views across Glaslyn to the summit of Yr Wyddfa, which still looks some way above. Stay with this and eventually you'll meet another path joining from the left. This is the Miners' Track and will be your return route. The junction is marked by a small standing stone.

Stay on the main path and start to climb up until a short steep section, which may require hands, leads onto a broad level saddle at Bwlch Glas. This is marked by a large standing stone. Turn left here and follow the path alongside the railway line. This rises sharply up to steps just below the summit. Climb these and enjoy the highest position in Wales.

To return, drop back down to the standing stone in Bwlch Glas, then descend the way you came up until you reach the path junction you passed earlier. Turn right here and drop steeply down to the shores of the beautiful Glaslyn, tucked beneath the mountain's steep northeast face.

Stay with the main path as it drops again and you'll soon reach the shores of Llyn Llydaw, where the gradient relents. All that's left now is an easy stroll out, following a good track and crossing a fine causeway to eventually reach the car park at the start.

◂ Yr Wyddfa above Glaslyn

Beddgelert Forest and Llyn Llywelyn

Distance **4km** Time **1 hour 30**
Terrain **clear well-surfaced forest tracks**
Map **OS Explorer OL17** Access **Sherpa'r Wyddfa bus to Beddgelert Forest from Beddgelert, Bangor and Caernarfon**

Beddgelert Forest is riddled with tracks and trails that offer almost endless walking possibilities. It's a stunning woodland, as notable for its turbulent rivers and streams as it is for its mix of deciduous woodland and conifers. The highlight is a beautiful mountain lake, Llyn Llywelyn, which is the focal point of this walk.

Leave the A4085 2km south of Rhyd Ddu and 3km north of Beddgelert at the national park sign for Coedwig Beddgelert and follow the track for 600m to the main car park. From here, walk beneath the large wooden arch next to the interpretation board and follow the path up and around to the right to cross the Welsh Highland Railway. The path continues easily from here, passing close to some atmospheric ruins and also offering access to one of the forest's many rivers, the Afon Cwm Du, via a narrow path on the left. It eventually climbs to meet a main forest track.

Turn left onto this, crossing the river, then turn right up a narrow path that climbs easily by another stream. This steepens near the top, eventually spilling out onto another broad forest track. Turn left and continue to a crossroads.

Keep ahead up a steep ramp onto another forest track and follow this easily through mixed woodland. Most of the climbing is in the bag at this stage so this track undulates sweetly along the contour lines, making for delightful walking.

At the next crossroads, keep straight ahead. The right turn also takes you to

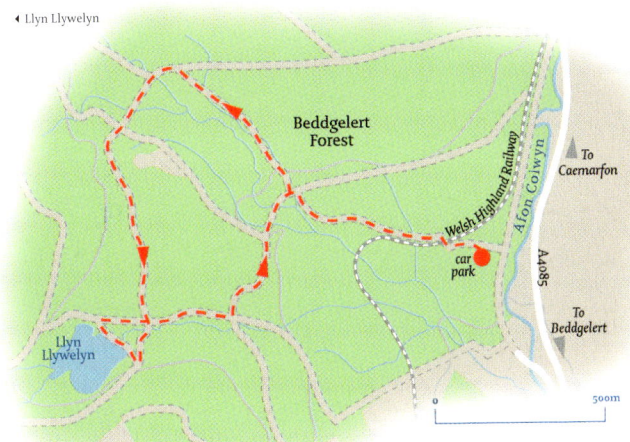

◀ Llyn Llywelyn

Llyn Llywelyn but this little loop is best walked clockwise. Climb steeply for a few paces and once you reach the banks of the lake, turn right onto a path that crosses the dam. By now, you have expansive views east across to the Yr Wyddfa massif.

There is something breathtakingly beautiful about Llyn Llywelyn, a natural mountain tarn which has been enlarged into a reservoir. Rugged hillsides drop to the glistening waters and the lofty summits of Moel Hebog, Moel yr Ogof and Moel Lefn provide a dramatic backdrop. A small tree-covered promontory reaches out into the waters at the far end of the dam.

From here, return to the path that crosses the dam and continue out onto a forest track. Anybody looking to extend the walk could now turn left and make a lap of the lake, adding another 1km to the total distance. Otherwise, turn right, drop down past the turning you exited from earlier, and continue steeply down to another crossroads, this one with stunning views ahead towards Yr Wyddfa and Yr Aran.

Turn left here to continue easily downwards, passing a large red boulder, to a junction. Keep right, still dropping easily, and you'll shortly pass on the left the entrance to the narrow path you walked up earlier. A few paces further on, you can turn right to drop onto your outward path, which you now follow easily back to the railway and the car park.

Cwm Bychan and Llyn Dinas

Distance 9km Time 4 hours
Terrain rough footpaths, steep ground;
easy return section Map OS Explorer OL17
Access Sherpa'r Wyddfa bus to Beddgelert
from Bangor, Caernarfon and Porthmadog

This route follows the course of the tumultuous Afon Glaslyn before leaving it at the Aberglaslyn Bridge to climb onto rough ground that feels way higher and more remote than it really is.

There are a few parking options in Beddgelert. Whichever you use, make your way to the bridge in the centre of the village and turn up the narrow lane on its south side, past the public toilets, keeping the Afon Colwyn to your left until you reach another bridge and the confluence with the Afon Glaslyn. Don't cross; instead turn right through a gate to follow the Afon Glaslyn beside meadows.

Soon after passing the church, a sign points right to Gelert's Grave, beyond which lies a statue of a dog (150m). This simple stone monument is said to mark the final resting place of Gelert, the loyal hound of medieval Welsh Prince Llywelyn the Great.

Back on the main route, the path eventually crosses a footbridge and then goes right to cross the railway, now keeping the river to the right. As you progress, the path is rougher and harder to walk until it becomes a narrow walkway squeezed between vertical rockfaces and the thundering waters. Fortunately there are handrails to assist here. The path passes a mineshaft – take a torch if you want to look inside – and then climbs onto easier ground amidst lovely deciduous woodland.

Before the bridge, turn left to climb over the hill and drop to the car park at Nantmor. Turn left in the car park and

Cwm Bychan and Llyn Dinas

◀ Llyn Dinas

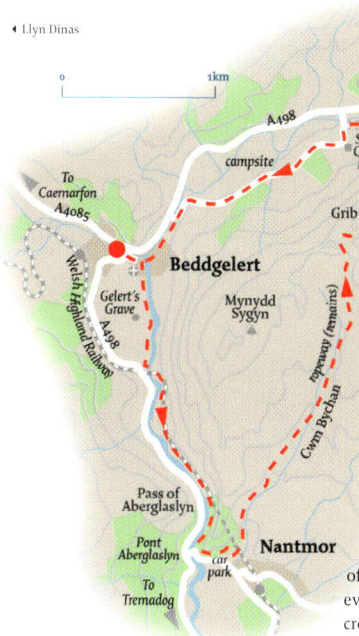

leave it at the top, past the picnic benches and up the hill. The path gradually climbs alongside the Nant Bychan, eventually crossing it and then passing the remains of the Cwm Bychan Copper Mine aerial ropeway, which would have been used to drop the copper ore down to Nantmor.

Shortly after the ropeway, you'll pass a path that leads left and a small waymark post. Ignore this but stay alert for another 50m, where you pass a pile of rocks and mining waste. Turn left immediately after this and clamber up a short steep faint path that takes you onto a much clearer grassy path. This now leads delightfully into a remote hanging cwm sheltering a small tarn.

Continue steeply upwards in a rocky bowl and then bear right to follow an unlikely path around the rim of the bowl, beneath steep crags, eventually emerging at a fence which you cross via a ladder stile. Continue past more mine ruins and old shafts, and follow the waymark arrow onto a narrow path towards Llyn Dinas.

This drops sharply down to the shores of the lake. Turn left and go through a gate, ignoring a bridge on your right to carry on along a clear path towards Beddgelert. On meeting the drive of the Sygun Copper Mine, turn left, then just before the mine entrance go right to follow a good path onto a lane. Continue down the valley, ignoring another bridge over the Afon Glaslyn to keep ahead on a footpath that leads back to the confluence of the two rivers in Beddgelert.

Craflwyn and Afon y Cwm

Distance 5km **Time** 2 hours
Terrain rough, occasionally muddy footpaths and some steep sections
Map OS Explorer OL17 **Access** Sherpa'r Wyddfa bus to the Craflwyn Hall entrance from Porthmadog and Beddgelert

This little gem of a walk starts by the National Trust-owned Craflwyn Hall and follows clear but rough and, in places, muddy paths steeply up onto seldom trodden ground high above the lovely valley of the Afon Glaslyn.

It offers fantastic views over the peaks of the Moelwynion mountain range and later of Yr Aran, at the southern end of Yr Wyddfa's south ridge. Lower down it winds through enchanting woodland, passing two waterfalls – one on the way up and both on the way down. Higher up, it weaves across rolling hillsides, passing the viewpoint of the Giant's Chair and crossing the tumbling Afon y Cwm.

Start at the Craflwyn Hall National Trust car park, which is on the A498 about 1.5km northeast of Beddgelert. Head out of the top of the car park and wind your way up through the woods above, ignoring junctions with narrower paths and following black arrows on marker posts. Pass the lower of the two waterfalls visited on this walk and then climb steeply on stone steps until it levels and you reach a junction with a rough path on the left that heads straight up the hillside. Leave the black arrows behind here and follow this path steeply uphill.

Continue out onto open ground and you'll soon come to the Giant's Chair – a great spot to stop and catch your breath while you soak up the stunning views. Once refreshed, head on up from here,

◀ Woodland above Craflwyn Hall

shortly crossing a stile and breaking left and then right to start a long traverse across the hillside. Continue to a ladder stile and then keep straight ahead again, with a fence to your right, to carry on around the hillside. This is a lovely section of the walk with great views and little in the way of up and down. You'll eventually pass a tumbledown building and come to another stile that leads to a bridge over the Afon y Cwm.

Cross the bridge and follow the track down to the right, keeping left at a fork soon afterwards. Continue downhill now, left first, then around a sharp right-hand bend, and down to a wall where you meet another track.

Turn right onto this and continue until you reach a footbridge that crosses the river again, this time by a wonderful waterfall. The path now heads back into woodland and continues to the junction where you turned off onto the rough path earlier. Stay with the main path and pass the first waterfall again before dropping back down to the Craflwyn Hall car park.

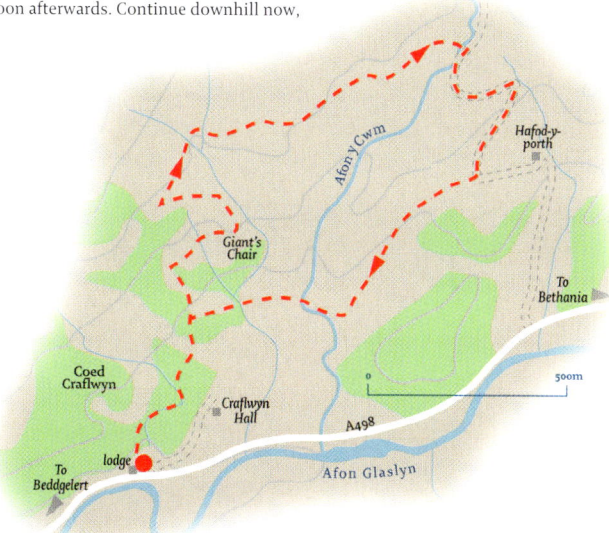

Llyn Gwynant

Distance 5km **Time** 1 hour 30
Terrain footpaths, with some boggy, awkward and rocky stretches; roadside section on a raised pavement to finish
Map OS Explorer OL17 **Access** Sherpa'r Wyddfa bus to Bryn Gwynant from Beddgelert and Porthmadog

The Afon Glaslyn rises up at the foot of Yr Wyddfa, and drops steeply into the Gwynant Valley, where it then swings south and tumbles easily down into the stunning Llyn Gwynant. At over 1km long, and covering an area of more than 120 acres, this is one of Eryri's larger lakes, as well as one of the most beautiful.

This short but quite tough walk loops around the lake, initially following the northern shores, then crossing the Afon Glaslyn to access a rough, rocky, wooded path that tracks high above the western shores. It then crosses the Afon Glaslyn again before taking the road easily back to the start.

There are limited parking bays at various points along the A948 which runs beside Llyn Gwynant, around 7km northeast of Beddgelert. Wherever you park, start by walking alongside the A948 with Llyn Gwynant to your left and continue until you reach a footpath sign that points you down to the lake shore. Cross a ladder stile and keep straight ahead around the head of the lake. Climb a short steep ramp and then drop to a beach, where you should look for a waymark directing you right into Llyn Gwynant Campsite.

Follow clear waymarks along a broad track that leads away from the lake and carry on through the campsite to cross a long footbridge over the Afon Glaslyn.

◀ Llyn Gwynant

Now follow the rough, rocky path through the woods. This drops and climbs a little at times, and eventually leads to another ladder stile.

Cross this and keep straight ahead, then after a short steep, rocky section, where hands may be needed, look out for a vague path to the right that climbs to the top of the wooded knoll you are on. The path soon improves and passes above some small cliffs. Stay with it to eventually leave the woodland and cross open ground to a gate. Keep straight ahead here, following a wall on your left briefly, and then drop down behind the trees to join the access track for Bwlch Mwlchan bunkhouse.

Turn right onto this and follow it to a gateway where you are funnelled into a narrow opening by a wall with the Afon Glaslyn on your left. Go over the old flagstone bridge and walk up through the field opposite to a stile. Cross this and climb to a gate that leads onto the road. Turn left and follow the pavement back to the lakeside and the start.

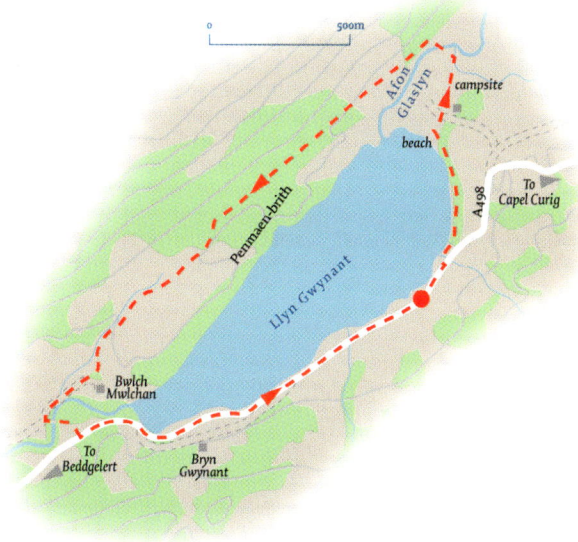

The Aberglaslyn Gorge

Distance 8km **Time** 2 hours 30
Terrain clear paths but they can be confusing in places; some steep sections and exposure near cliff edges
Map OS Explorer OL17 **Access** Sherpa'r Wyddfa bus to Beddgelert from Bangor, Caernarfon and Porthmadog

Although it covers the same ground as the start of the Cwm Bychan and Llyn Dinas route, this is a much shorter, notably easier walk that enables less fit or experienced walkers the opportunity to explore the dramatic Aberglaslyn Gorge.

A short section on a narrow and often busy road can be avoided by simply reversing the outward leg if you prefer – it's the gorge and the wonderful fisherman's path that provide the highlights of the walk. The Afon Glaslyn is a stunning river – perhaps Eryri's most spectacular – and nowhere is it more dramatic than on the short stretch that runs alongside the Welsh Highland Railway to Pont Aberglaslyn. The view back from the bridge must be one of the finest in the national park.

There are a few parking options in Beddgelert. Whichever you use, make your way to the bridge in the centre of the village and turn up the narrow lane on its south side, past the public toilets, keeping the Afon Colwyn to your left until you reach an iron bridge and the confluence with the Afon Glaslyn. Cross the bridge and turn right on the far bank to leave the village green and pretty cottages behind and walk downstream, now with the river on your right.

The path is well-surfaced and easy to follow and the river, while fairly quiet on this stretch, still provides plenty to look at. It's a great place to spot dippers and herons, and maybe even the odd

THE ABERGLASLYN GORGE

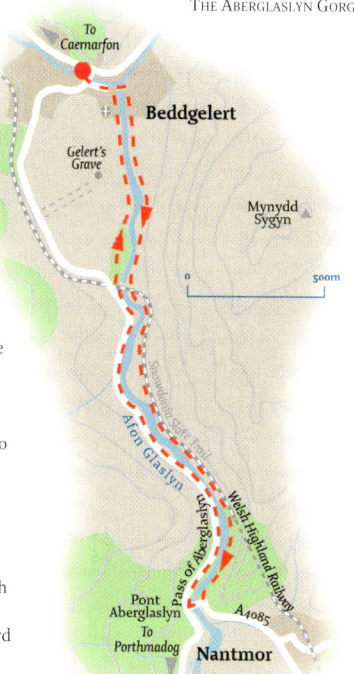

◀ Bridge over the Afon Colwyn in Beddgelert

goosander. Continue through a couple of gates and beneath some steep boulder-strewn hillsides until you eventually reach a path junction, a footbridge and a railway bridge. For a short walk, you can cross the bridge here and return to Beddgelert on the other bank of the river.

For the full route, turn left to cross the railway, and then drop down to a rocky outcrop. A narrow path leads down to a lovely pebble beach, or you can keep ahead with the river now further away to your right for a few minutes. Continue as the path rejoins the riverbank and soon becomes stony and starts to undulate. The steps get more awkward the further you get.

The next section is spectacular, though also exposed and difficult, with rails on the rock to help you around one awkward corner and steps on one slabby section. Keep ahead and you'll drop to pass a mineshaft – a torch is needed if you wish to look inside – and then into woodland, where a few more ups and downs lead to Pont Aberglaslyn.

Go through the gate onto the road and cross the bridge before turning right to climb uphill on the pavement. This tapers away further up and you need to walk on the road, facing the oncoming traffic, until a gap in the wall to your right gives access to a rough path. Now follow this, parallel to the wall, and keep ahead for around 1km until a steep awkward section leads to a stile. Cross and keep ahead on a rough, steep and slippery path that leads to a gate on the left and a better path. Turn right onto this and drop below the bridges before bearing left to climb up and join the obvious path. Turn right onto this and follow it back towards Beddgelert with the river on your right. An optional path leads left to Gelert's Grave, a memorial to Llywelyn the Great's faithful hound whose sacrifice, legend has it, accounts for Beddgelert's name.

Croesor to Cnicht

Distance 12km **Time** 4 hours
Terrain rough mountain paths, some short sections where hands may be required and one section crossing boggy ground on a vague path where careful navigation is needed **Maps** OS Explorer OL17 and OL18
Access no public transport to the start

Small but perfectly formed, Cnicht is a mountain that should appear on every walker's hit list. It is often referred to as the Welsh Matterhorn, and from Cwm Croesor it's easy to see why.

But, in fact, the mountain is more of a slender ridge that rises from a boggy plateau. And whilst it is a challenging climb to the summit, it's one that's well within reach of a fit hillwalker who doesn't mind using their hands on a few short steps. Whilst this isn't a long walk, it's definitely a tough one and with some awkward navigation in the middle, it's best saved for a good day.

Start at the small Cnicht car park just northwest of the little crossroads in the village of Croesor. From the back of the car park, cross the footbridge and turn left to the road. You'll see this is signed Snowdonia Slate Trail – much of the walk follows this long-distance footpath. Turn right to climb out of the village and follow the road to its end. Continue straight ahead through the gate and along the rough track, and at the top bear right through another gate, again well signed, to head almost directly towards Cnicht's distinctive summit.

Stay with the obvious but rough path to a small ruined building, where you turn right to a stile. Cross and keep ahead, eventually crossing another stile where the path turns rocky and narrow as it flanks a hill to the right. This leads back onto the crest of the ridge which you now follow, mainly on a clear path that leads to a broad grassy notch with a steep slab

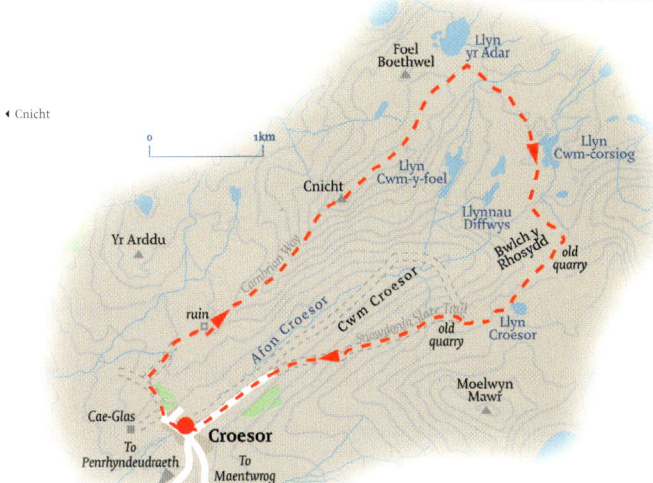

◀ Cnicht

ahead. A rough, steep path leads up to the right of this. Take this, using your hands in places, and then continue more easily to the first of Cnicht's tops which, at 689m, is the true summit and offers superb views over Moelwyn Mawr, as well as the rest of the walk.

Now keep straight ahead over two subsidiary summits before dropping to a fork. Bear left to take the best path towards Llyn yr Adar and, as you approach this, keep your eyes open for a cairn where you must turn right onto a narrow and rough path that now leads across boggy ground towards the quarry ruins at Bwlch y Rhosydd. Stay with the path as best you can – it is vague and boggy in places, but keep Llyn Cwm-corsiog in sight to your left and you'll meet a wire fence.

Follow this to the right and stay with it – you can walk on either side, though keeping it on your right is slightly clearer, until it drops to the quarry ruins and meets a broad quarry track. Turn right – Slate Trail waymark – and then keep left to loop around the last of the buildings. Now look for a small wooden post on the hillside above to your right. Once located, climb to this and follow a succession of yellow-topped posts over the hilltop and eventually up to the dam of Llyn Croesor. Cross this and stay with the path as it climbs a little higher, then drops to the disused Croesor Quarry. Cross the quarry and go over a stile on the far side. This leads onto a clear, broad track that you now follow back down to Croesor.

Keep ahead on the road until a sign directs you right past a house and into the rear of the car park.

Betws-y-Coed's position on the eastern boundary of the national park makes it the first real village visitors pass through if approaching along the historic coach road now known as the A5. The village also sits on the confluence of the Afon Conwy and the Afon Llugwy and at the entrance to the lovely Gwydir Forest.

Climbing into the mountains from here, you quickly reach Capel Curig, a hub for outdoor activities. For sheer drama, the horseshoe of Moel Siabod tops the list as a true mountain walk despite its modest height in comparison to its better-known neighbours.

A lower, more sheltered walk, perfect for a bad weather day, explores the old coaching road, now a rough track, passing the National Outdoor Centre at Plas y Brenin, and offering the best views anywhere of the Yr Wyddfa Horseshoe.

The longer outing that hurdles the hills between Llyn Geirionydd and Llyn Crafnant is probably the finest in this chapter and does a great job of linking two stunning lakes.

A delightful route from Trefriw skirts the northern fringes of the Gwydir Forest with memorable mountain views, while steep gradients lead from Betws-y-Coed to the enchanting Llyn Elsi hidden high above the village. For easier exploration, the short riverside walk from Betws-y-Coed offers up wildlife-sighting opportunities and can be linked with the cascades at Pont y Pair. To head away from it all, you can set out from historic Dolwyddelan for an all-weather walk into slate-mining country.

Around Betws-y-Coed

1. **Moel Siabod** — 36
   Escape the crowds drawn to the region's better-known peaks for this satisfying high circuit

2. **Capel Curig** — 38
   Take a lower-level tour of woodland and hillside from the famed outdoor centre and enjoy some classic views

3. **Llyn Geirionydd and Llyn Crafnant** — 40
   Walk in the footsteps of a celebrated Brittonic poet on this exploration of a pair of attractive lakes

4. **Trefriw and Llanrhychwyn** — 42
   Make a short but steep pilgrimage to what is thought to be the oldest standing church in Wales

5. **Dolwyddelan and Cwm Penamnen** — 44
   Follow a tumbling river through Llywelyn the Great's backyard and an old slate-mining heartland

6. **Betws-y-Coed two rivers walk** — 46
   Look out for dippers, kingfishers and leaping salmon on this easy-going riverside loop

7. **Betws-y-Coed and Llyn Elsi** — 48
   Leave the tourist hubbub behind for this initially very steep hike which takes you to a beautiful lake surrounded by woodland

Moel Siabod

Distance 10km **Time** 3-4 hours
Terrain mix of good paths, rough boggy paths and the occasional rocky step
Map OS Explorer OL17 **Access** buses from Betws-y-Coed, Corwen, Caernarfon, Llanberis and Bangor to Cyfyng Falls, Capel Curig, 300m from the start

Moel Siabod towers high above the A5 and the village of Capel Curig. At 872m, it misses out on Welsh 3000 status and, with this, the associated masses. Yet it's perfectly placed for sweeping views of Yr Wyddfa and Y Glyderau and is often quiet when its neighbours are teeming.

This walk approaches from the A5 east of Capel Curig, making a logical and highly enjoyable circuit of the mountain's steep-sided eastern cwm. It's a varied outing with close-up views of long-deserted slateworks, before clambering up an airy ridge crest to a rocky summit. The views in all directions are stunning, so allow time to take them all in.

Start at the Bryn Glo car park on the A5, 2km southeast of Capel Curig's centre. Cross the road to follow the pavement back towards Capel Curig, before turning left to cross the Pont Cyfyng, which gives great views over the cascading Afon Llugwy below. Continue up the lane, ignoring a tarmac track with a footpath sign on the right, and once opposite a row of cottages turn right up a narrow tarmac lane. This climbs steeply up through woodland to a sharp right-hand bend

MOEL SIABOD

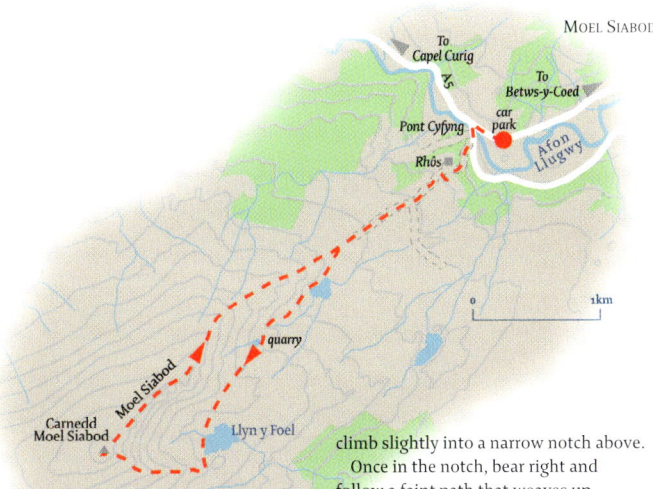

where you should keep straight ahead along a waymarked path, shortly rejoining the track above farm buildings. Continue to the left, soon crossing a stile and then ignoring a track to the left, to a ladder stile at the nose of the northeast ridge.

Follow a good rocky track straight ahead into the deep cwm that defines the eastern flanks of the mountain. Pass a lake to your left and stay on the path to climb slightly to some deserted quarry buildings. Pass these and then veer left to stay well above a dramatic water-filled pit. Keep straight ahead, with a steeper slope to your right, and you'll soon see the steely grey waters of Llyn y Foel directly ahead. Head for the southern tip of the lake, keeping the waters to your left, and upon reaching this go straight ahead to climb slightly into a narrow notch above.

Once in the notch, bear right and follow a faint path that weaves up through the heather. At this stage you have a choice: the main path runs parallel to the ridge, keeping a few metres below the craggy crest the whole way; or, for a more interesting alternative, it's possible to actually follow the crest in a series of optional easy yet exposed scrambles. Either way, you'll soon arrive at the summit which is marked by a trig point hidden among a jumble of rocks and boulders.

To descend, keep the cliffs of the steep-sided cwm to your right and head northeast. You'll soon locate a reasonably clear path that runs right around the escarpment edge. Follow this down and eventually the rock gives way to grass before finally meeting a tumbledown wall. Continue to a ladder stile. Cross this and trend rightwards to rejoin your outward route. Now retrace your steps to the start.

◀ Moel Siabod

Capel Curig

Distance 4.5km Time 2 hours
Terrain good paths and tracks throughout but a few busy road crossings
Map OS Explorer OL17 Access buses to Capel Curig from Betws-y-Coed, Llanberis, Corwen, Caernarfon and Bangor

While well-known as an outdoor hub, the village of Capel Curig is little more than a cluster of houses, hotels, pubs and cafés huddled around Thomas Telford's historic London to Holyhead Road – now known as the A5. This walk starts at the north end of the village to explore open hillside and woodland, never climbing high but offering fine panoramas of some of the most dramatic peaks in the area, including perhaps the most famous view of Yr Wyddfa – from the banks of Llynnau Mymbyr close to the National Outdoor Centre at Plas y Brenin.

Start at the car park at the north end of the village. Turn right out of the car park and follow the surfaced track, which is actually the old A5 road, through a gate by a cattle grid and on through another gate. Beyond this, turn immediately left – slightly uphill for a few paces – and keep ahead as the initially grassy track becomes a more established rocky track. Stay with this until it joins the main road, close to Plas y Brenin.

Cross the road, turn left, then turn right through a gate to walk down steps to a bridge at the outflow of Llynnau Mymbyr. On a clear day, this is one of the best places in the park to appreciate the size and grandeur of Yr Wyddfa. Cross the bridge and climb up to join a forest track where you turn left. Now follow this easily around the edge of the forest, passing through a gate, until you come

◀ Looking across Llynnau Mymbyr to Yr Wyddfa

to a T-junction. Turn left here and walk up, over another bridge, to join the A5. Turn right, then turn left up a driveway, forking right over a cattle grid, soon passing a row of houses. A short way further on, head around to the left and continue, passing a house on your right. Keep straight ahead, staying on the waymarked bridleway, until you see a gate on your right.

Go through this, enter a small copse, then go through another gate onto open ground. Follow the path as it twists and turns its way to a wooden footbridge. Don't cross; instead turn left onto the stone path and follow this as it runs beneath the rocky turret of Clogwyn Mawr. Pass through a succession of gates, all the time staying on the main path, and after a couple of small climbs and drops, you'll wind your way down to a pasture.

Follow the obvious track down round the right-hand side of the field to arrive at the A5, close to the car park.

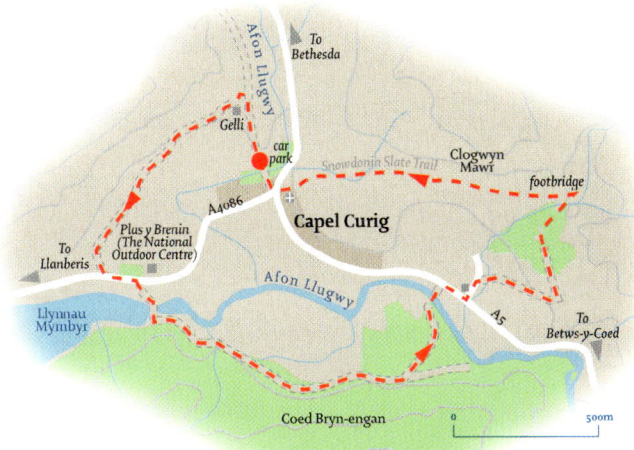

AROUND BETWS-Y-COED

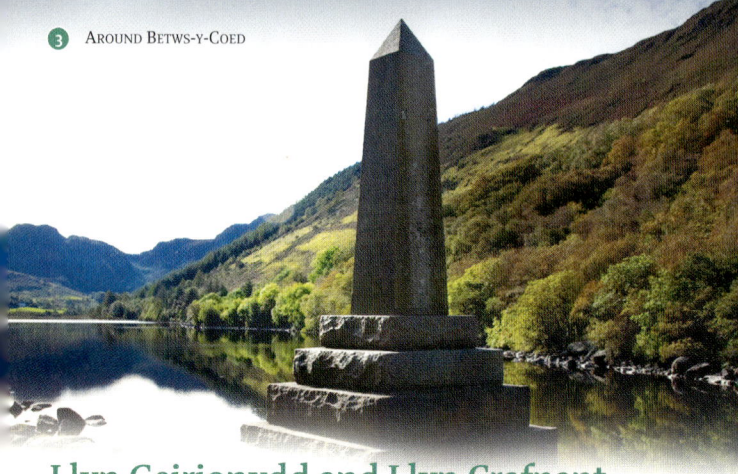

Llyn Geirionydd and Llyn Crafnant

Distance **8.5km** Time **3 hours**
Terrain **forest tracks and rough footpaths; very steep in places** Map **OS Explorer OL17**
Access **no public transport to the start**

This walk is perhaps the ultimate exploration of the Gwydir Forest, linking two stunningly beautiful but very different lakes with a mix of forest tracks and rough and ready footpaths.

Llyn Geirionydd has a significant past and its shores are thought to have been where the 6th-century poet, Taliesin, lived. You'll pass a stone monument to him at the tip of the lake. Llyn Crafnant is actually a reservoir, though this does little to distract from its beauty, tucked beneath rugged slopes at the foot of the Carneddau mountains. In the 19th century, the area was very much more industrial, and you'll pass tips and disused quarries on the walk.

The 5km of single-track road to Llyn Geirionydd is signed off the A5 about halfway between Capel Curig and Betws-y-Coed. From the car park at the southern end of the lake, start the walk by turning left back onto the road and walking past the end of the lake to a forest track on your right. Go around the barrier and walk up the forest track, passing the lake, then bearing left to climb slightly, still on a forest track. Continue up, around a right-hand bend, then around a left-hand bend, ignoring a track to the right. A few paces further on, turn right onto a narrow footpath and climb a little more steeply to rejoin the forest track.

Turn right, then immediately left, before keeping directly ahead onto a footpath where the forest track bears around to the right again. Follow this up and then down towards Llyn Crafnant. On reaching a wall at the bottom of the

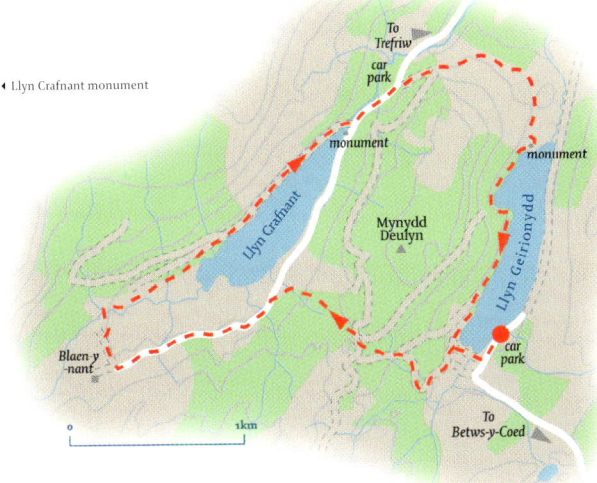

◀ Llyn Crafnant monument

forest, turn left to continue down, over a stream, and out onto a road.

Turn left to start the loop of Llyn Crafnant and follow the lane to its end, where you go through a gate and then turn right. Follow this over a footbridge and around to the right to join a forest track. Keep ahead, with Llyn Crafnant to your right, and follow the track all the way to the northern tip of the lake.

Cross the bridge, pass the monument, then turn left onto the road and follow it down until you reach a wide forest track to your right. Take this and climb to a broad open area, where the track bears right. You need to keep straight ahead on a narrow footpath that leads to a stile.

The path is now rough in places. Bear right at a fork almost immediately, then again at another. Climb to a gap in a wall, where you keep left, and then drop to a ladder stile, which you cross (doggy gate to the right). Keep ahead and then follow the path rightwards and uphill.

From the crest of the hill, drop towards Llyn Geirionydd with the Taliesin Monument looking down over the water. Turn left onto a broad track which leads down to the shore. Go right to continue through a gate and around the shore.

After a small beach, the path rises steeply and awkwardly into the woods for a few metres. Stay with it as it levels again before dropping steeply. Turn right onto a broad path and follow this easily with the lake down to your left. At a fork, keep left to drop to the shore and cross a meadow to rejoin the outward track. Turn left onto this and left onto the road to finish.

Trefriw and Llanrhychwyn

Distance 6km Time 2 hours
Terrain clear footpaths, farm tracks and quiet lanes; a short section on a busy road at the start/finish Map OS Explorer OL17
Access bus to Trefriw from Llandudno, Betws-y-Coed and Conwy

Llanrhychwyn Church, known locally as Llywelyn's Church, is thought to be the oldest standing church in Wales, with some of its structure originally dating back as far as the 11th century. The ancient church forms the focal point of this short but steep walk which starts in the small village of Trefriw, close to the Afon Conwy.

This walk climbs steeply into the nearby hills via a spectacular path that traces the line of the tumbling Afon Crafnant and passes some impressive waterfalls along the way. The hilltop section threads an enjoyable line through some fine deciduous woodland with great views over the nearby high mountains. Although short, it's quite steep in places so allow plenty of time.

Parking can be found on Gower Road opposite the Woollen Mill. Head back out onto the B5106 and turn right. Cross the bridge, then turn left up a steep hill. Turn almost immediately left again onto a narrow path that runs above the Afon Crafnant. Continue up to the Fairy Falls, passing a bridge, then double back to cross the bridge, turning right on the other side to climb to a road, School Hill.

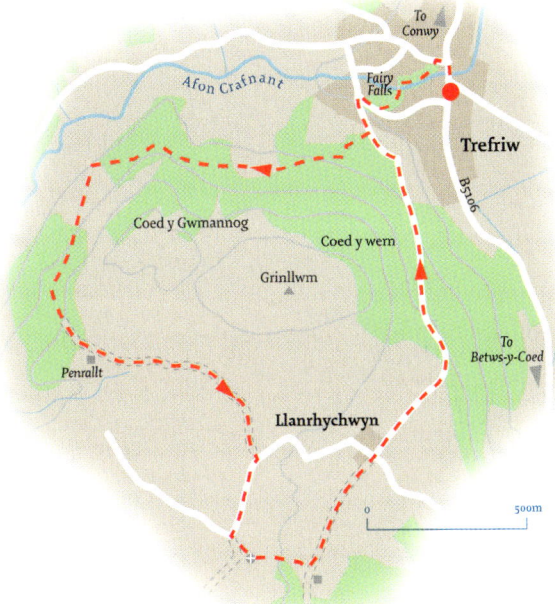

Turn right to a junction with Trefriw Road, then go left to follow this lane uphill to a footpath at a lay-by on the right. Follow this into the woods and climb through trees, then out onto open hillside, with fine views over the high mountains of Eryri. Stay with the path as it continues to an even better viewpoint, then fork left and clamber up to a stile.

Pass to the right of a house and join a track which you now follow straight ahead through a series of gates. Continue to a junction with a narrow lane and turn right. Follow this, keeping left at the next junction, and then look out for a signposted walkers' gate on the left when the track bends again. Go across the field to explore the beautiful old Llanrhychwyn Church, with its ancient oak door and beams, if it's unlocked.

From the church, keep the fence to your right and continue to a gate. Go through and drop through a succession of gates and down steps to meet a track at the bottom. Turn left to a crossroads and keep straight ahead to walk downhill on a narrow lane. This returns you to your outward route, which you can now follow back down past the Fairy Falls into Trefriw.

◀ Above the Afon Crafnant

Dolwyddelan and Cwm Penamnen

Distance 3.5km **Time** 1 hour 30
Terrain quiet lanes and forest tracks
Map OS Explorer OL17 **Access** trains
to Dolwyddelan from Llandudno,
Betws-y-Coed and Blaenau Ffestiniog

The small village of Dolwyddelan has
a fascinating past that belies its small size.
Llywelyn the Great, the medieval ruler
who dominated Wales for half a century,
is thought to have been born in the
nearby timber and stone keep known as
Tomen Castell, just west of the village.
He later went on to build the more
impressive Castell Dolwyddelan which
looms over the A470, not far away. Fans
of the cult 1980s Disney film Dragonslayer
may recognise it as Castle Morgenthorme
whose inhabitants were terrorised by
Vermithrax Pejorative, a fearsome 400-
year-old dragon.

The village sits astride the Afon Lledr,
which tumbles down from the nearby
Moelwynion mountain range, though this
walk explores one of the river's tributaries
– the Afon Cwm Penamnen, which rises
up close to some of the area's most
impressive historic slate quarries. It is an
easy walk, both short and mainly level,
following good surfaces the whole way
around, making it ideal if the weather is a
little too wild for the mountains.

Turn left out of Dolwyddelan Station
car park onto the road and pass the school
to continue to a junction. Turn left to
cross the bridge over the railway and then
keep left again into the High Street. Pass a
turning for Rathbone Terrace on the right,
then take the next, continuing past a few
new houses to join a forest track.

The navigation is finished for a while
now as you keep straight ahead to climb

◀ Ruins of Tai Penamnen

the track into Cwm Penamnen, with the Afon Cwm Penamnen way down to your right. Carry on to a fork and keep right to continue more easily to another junction, where a waymark points you down to the right, off the main track.

This leads down to a footbridge that spans the Afon Cwm Penamnen. Cross, then continue up to a tarmac lane – this is Sarn Helen, a Roman Road that runs the length of Wales from near Swansea to the North Wales coast.

Turn right onto this and follow it easily back down the valley, shortly passing the fascinating remnants of Tai Penamnen where an information board explains some of the history of the ruins. Continue down the valley and you'll eventually arrive back at the railway bridge you crossed earlier.

Cross again and turn right to return to the car park or continue straight ahead to visit the centre of Dolwyddelan where there is a shop and a good pub.

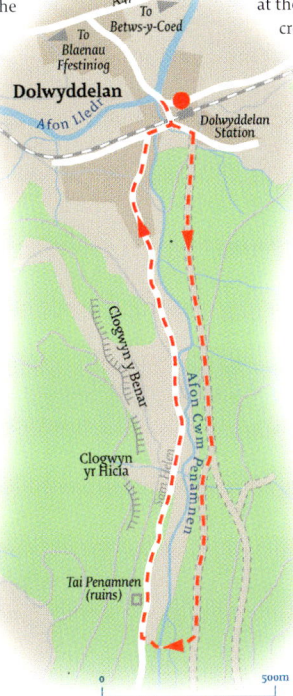

Betws-y-Coed two rivers walk

Distance 2km **Time** 1 hour
Terrain mainly level paths, some muddy sections with a small section on a lane
Map OS Explorer OL17 **Access** trains to Betws-y-Coed from Llandudno and Blaenau Ffestiniog; buses from Llandudno, Bangor and Caernarfon

This is the easiest walk in this guide and one of the loveliest. It follows the course of the Afon Llugwy, which drops from the mountains to the west above Capel Curig, and then later, the Afon Conwy – a magnificent waterway that rises to the south in a little known pocket of upland known as the Migneint.

It provides a perfect focal point for a visit to the village, and is also a great place to spot herons, dippers and kingfishers. Keen eyes might catch the odd trout or salmon jumping from the crystal-clear waters.

This route starts from the short-stay car park opposite the railway station. Adjacent to the north entrance to the car park, follow a surfaced path to the old stables, with the playing field to your left, and then turn right as if to walk around the far end of the stables, until you see a large wooden gate ahead on your left.

Go through this and follow a tarmac track easily along, passing a succession of houses and shortly joining the Afon Llugwy on your left. With the navigation over for a while, continue with the river to your left, head beneath the railway bridge and continue to hug the banks of the Afon Llugwy, soon passing the golf course to your right.

Stay with the path and you'll shortly come to the confluence of the two mighty rivers, marked by a perfectly-placed park bench. You are effectively turning right here to now follow the Afon Conwy

◀ The Afon Llugwy

upstream, still with the golf course on your right. This is a wonderful stretch with the river to your left overhung by shrubs and small trees that are usually brimming with birdlife.

Continue easily, following any signage that aims to protect you from wayward golf balls and eventually, after passing a few interesting flood defence weirs, you'll be funnelled into a narrow tree-lined section, with the golf clubhouse to your right. Keep your eyes to the water for any signs of birds or fish, as the route then ushers you onto a lane at the entrance to the clubhouse. Keep ahead here, then bear around to the right with a cemetery to your left.

Stay with the lane to pass a caravan park entrance to your right before bending back left with the Conwy Valley Railway Museum and then Betws-y-Coed railway station to your right. Go right through a gate to cross the footbridge over the tracks and return to the start.

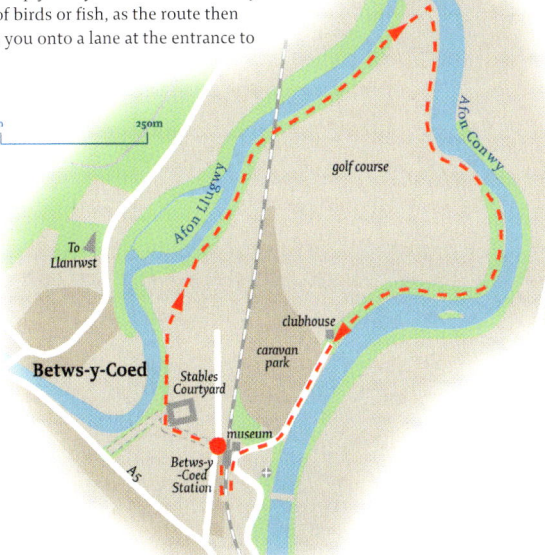

Around Betws-y-Coed

Betws-y-Coed and Llyn Elsi

Distance 5.9km **Time** 2 hours
Terrain forest tracks and rough footpaths.
Very steep in places **Map** OS Explorer OL17
Access trains to Betws-y-Coed from
Llandudno and Blaenau Ffestiniog; buses
from Llandudno, Bangor and Caernarfon

Betws-y-Coed, the self-proclaimed
'Y Porth i Eryri' (Gateway to Snowdonia),
is a bustling but lovely village sitting on
the confluence of the Afon Llugwy and
the Afon Conwy. It's a tourist haven with
cafés, pubs and an abundance of outdoor
shops, and there's plenty to see here too,
with the impressive Church of St Mary
and the dramatic cascades and rapids in
the Afon Llugwy as it runs beneath Pont-
y-Pair – the Bridge of the Cauldron.

Both sides of the Llugwy Valley are
steep and wooded and this walk explores
the southern slopes, starting at the small
railway station. From here, walk back out
to the main A5 road and turn right, then
first left after the shops to climb steeply
up the road behind St Mary's Church. Bear
around to the right and turn left onto a
forest track, following the white arrow
markers for the Llyn Elsi Walk.

The next section is incredibly steep but
there are resting posts and benches
spaced evenly to allow you to catch your
breath. Make your way slowly uphill,
passing footpaths to your left and right,
and then after the gradient finally relents,
keep right at a fork in the forest track –
still following the arrow waymarks.

The going is much easier here, so enjoy
the walking and the woodland and you
soon come to another track junction
where you turn right again, and then
another, where you bear left.

At the next track junction, keep straight

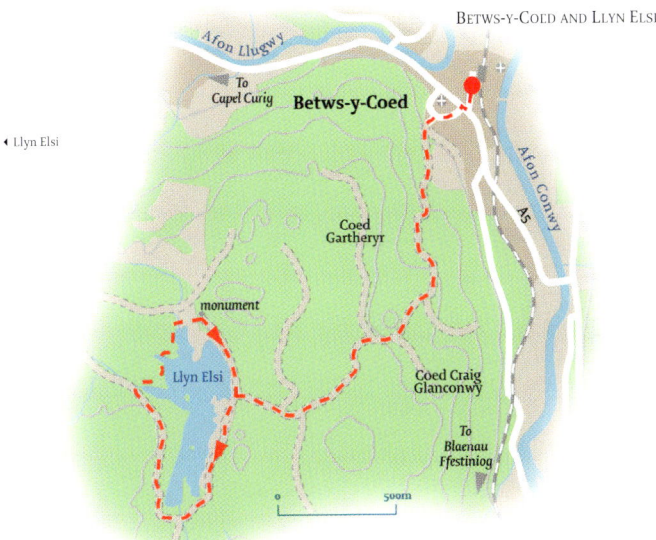

◀ Llyn Elsi

ahead with a track going left. Further on, at a T-junction, turn left to continue, now on level ground, to the shores of Llyn Elsi. Stay with the track as it continues easily around the southern tip of the lake and ignore a turning on the left to carry on up the western shore, still on a good track. The views are stunning and they get better.

The track curves around to the left to sweep around a deep inlet where a small stream enters the lake; bear right here onto a narrow path that crosses a footbridge over the stream. Continue around the shore of the lake before crossing the dam and climbing to the monument which commemorates the opening of Betws-y-Coed waterworks in 1914. Before it was dammed, this was actually two smaller lakes – Llyn Rhisgog and Llyn Enoc. It marks a fantastic viewpoint with the lake stretched out ahead of you and beyond that the rugged hills of the Moelwynion massif. Interestingly, during the Second World War, evacuees based in the area would swim out to the islands in the lake to supplement their rations with gulls' eggs. The gulls are still here.

From the monument, continue around the lake on a good forest track and, at the next junction, turn left on the forest road followed earlier to start the long descent back to the village. The going is much easier on the way down and you don't have to worry about navigation, so enjoy the scenery and continue back down into Betws-y-Coed where a choice of refreshments awaits.

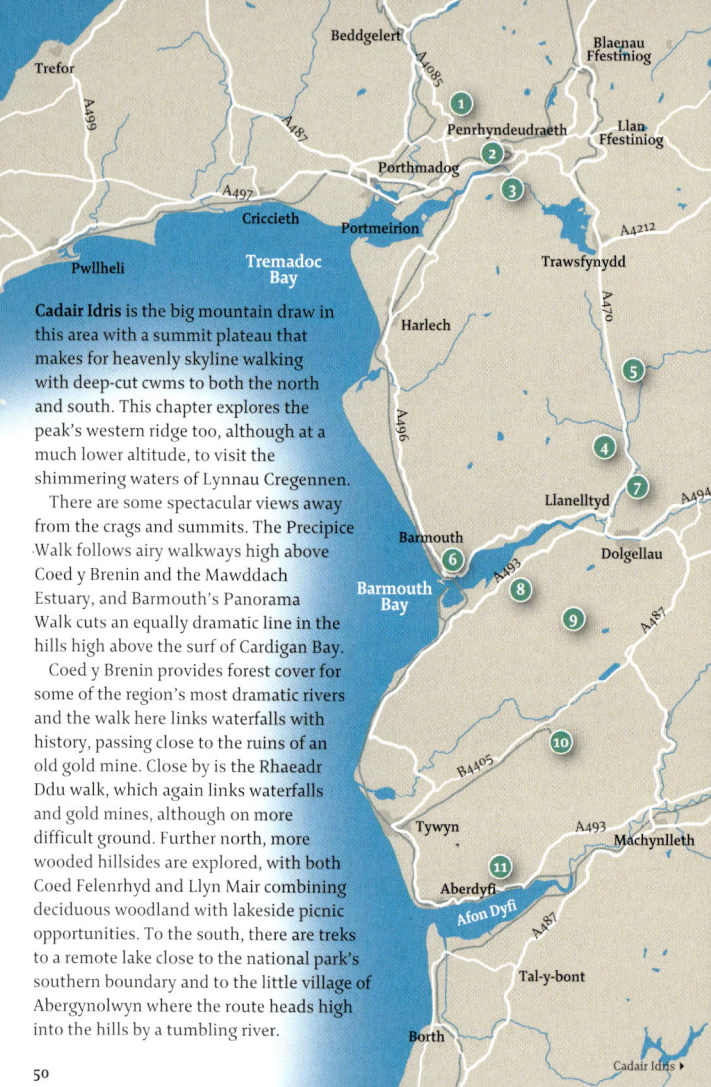

Cadair Idris is the big mountain draw in this area with a summit plateau that makes for heavenly skyline walking with deep-cut cwms to both the north and south. This chapter explores the peak's western ridge too, although at a much lower altitude, to visit the shimmering waters of Lynnau Cregennen.

There are some spectacular views away from the crags and summits. The Precipice Walk follows airy walkways high above Coed y Brenin and the Mawddach Estuary, and Barmouth's Panorama Walk cuts an equally dramatic line in the hills high above the surf of Cardigan Bay.

Coed y Brenin provides forest cover for some of the region's most dramatic rivers and the walk here links waterfalls with history, passing close to the ruins of an old gold mine. Close by is the Rhaeadr Ddu walk, which again links waterfalls and gold mines, although on more difficult ground. Further north, more wooded hillsides are explored, with both Coed Felenrhyd and Llyn Mair combining deciduous woodland with lakeside picnic opportunities. To the south, there are treks to a remote lake close to the national park's southern boundary and to the little village of Abergynolwyn where the route heads high into the hills by a tumbling river.

Southern Eryri

1. **Croesor from Pont Garreg-Hylldrem** 52
   Follow the course of two rivers on this easy hillside circuit

2. **Llyn Mair and Llyn Hafod-y-llyn** 54
   Take in two beautifully-situated lakes and a superb viewpoint

3. **Coed Felenrhyd** 56
   Start with a nature reserve tour before hiking to an upland reservoir

4. **Coed Ganllwyd and Rhaeadr Ddu** 58
   Climb from the dramatic Black Waterfall to visit an old gold mine

5. **Coed y Brenin** 60
   Dive deep into the King's Forest to discover some magnificent waterfalls and industrial ruins

6. **Above Barmouth** 62
   All the effort is well rewarded with wonderful views on this tough circuit

7. **Precipice Walk** 64
   Not as scary as it sounds – but plenty of exposure and lofty views

8. **Llynnau Cregennen** 66
   From the lakeside, head up the flank of an attractive hill to enjoy the views

9. **Cadair Idris** 68
   Pass two lovely mountain lakes on a steepening approach to a celebrated summit viewpoint

10. **Nant Gwernol** 70
    Hike up alongside a cascading river before exploring an old slate quarry

11. **Llyn Barfog** 72
    King Arthur's horse left its mark on this excellent circuit which takes in a remote mountain lake

Croesor from Pont Garreg-Hylldrem

Distance 6km Time 2 hours 30
Terrain clear paths, though some muddy, and a short section on a quiet lane
Map OS Explorer OL18 Access no public transport to the start

This walk follows two small rivers that both rise up in the Moelwynion mountain range and join forces close to the start at Pont Garreg-Hylldrem before emptying into the Afon Glaslyn just a few miles further downstream.

It is definitely a walk of two halves, with the outward leg climbing high above the valley to follow a lovely ridgeline with views up to the pointed summit of Cnicht, while the return leg stays in the cover of majestic beech and other trees before finishing on sheep pasture.

Start from the lay-by just west of Pont Garreg-Hylldrem on the A4085 between Beddgelert and Penrhyndeudraeth. Walk towards the bridge but instead of crossing it, keep straight ahead through a gate beside a cattle grid, signposted as a private road. This leads easily alongside the Afon Croesor. Pass a house on your left and bear slightly left to climb above another. Then bear left to climb steeply up through the wood, going left at the top, with crags to your right.

Pass the end of the crags and follow the path around to the right to now walk along the ridgetop above them. The waymarked path is clear and the going is easy with soft grass beneath your feet for the most part and fine views towards Cnicht and Moelwyn Mawr, as well as the Yr Wyddfa range to the left.

Continue through gates until, with a house directly in front, you are directed right, through a gate in the wall. Once through keep left to walk above the house and then stay high, with the

CROESOR FROM PONT GARREG-HYLLDREM

◀ Cnicht from Pont Garreg-Hylldrem

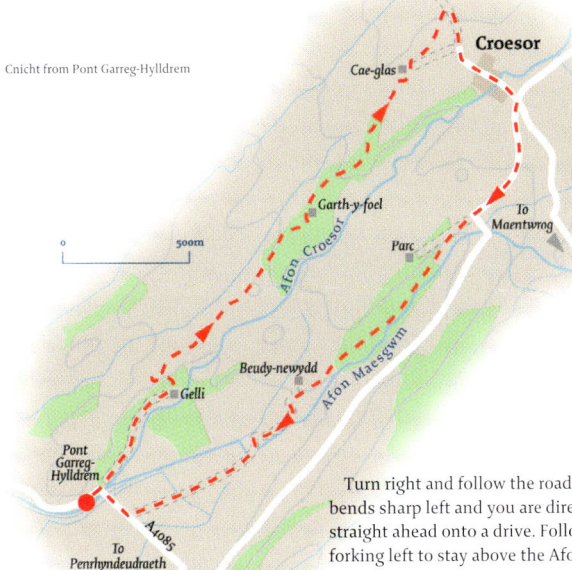

outbuildings to your left, to continue up onto rough ground.

Stay with the path the whole time and you eventually reach the large white house of Cae-glas, an early example of a 16th-century Snowdonian house and thought to be one of the first storeyed houses in Wales. Go through a succession of gates to reach a ladder stile and a stony track beyond Cae-glas. Follow this down and go through a gate to join the top of the road above Croesor village. Walk down into the village and pass the Cnicht car park to reach a crossroads.

Turn right and follow the road until it bends sharp left and you are directed straight ahead onto a drive. Follow this, forking left to stay above the Afon Maesgwm, and then continue along the track, which can get wet and muddy, until it goes through a gate and emerges into the open, with a grass-topped slate mound ahead.

Keep to the top of the mound for a few paces and then drop to the right to join a track on the right. Follow this down and around left- and right-hand bends to continue to a bridge that leads onto open sheep pasture. Cross the bridge and turn right to follow the bank that accompanies the river around a left-hand bend before continuing to a gate close to Pont Garreg-Hylldrem. Go onto the road and turn right to cross the bridge to the start.

Llyn Mair and Llyn Hafod-y-llyn

Distance 5km Time 2 hours
Terrain good footpaths and forest tracks with a few steep awkward sections
Map OS Explorer OL18 Access no public transport to the start

This walk links the tranquil waters of Llyn Mair and Llyn Hafod-y-llyn, two beautiful hidden lakes created in 1889 by William Edward Oakeley, the then owner of nearby Plas Tan-y-bwlch, as a 21st-birthday present for his daughter Mair. They were also used as a water supply and to drive a small hydro-electric scheme, which provided Plas Tan-y-bwlch with what is believed to be the first electric lighting in North Wales.

From the car park off the B4410, about 300m west of the entrance road to the Ffestiniog Railway at Tan-y-Bwlch, continue along the forest road and through the gate. Keep ahead until you see a narrow path on the left. Take this and walk along the wooded shores of Llyn Hafod-y-llyn. This then climbs away from the lake before dropping to the dam at the southern end. Keep ahead over this and turn right onto a forest track.

Pass a house on the left, then turn left at a footpath sign to join a terrace path with fantastic views. Stay with this until you reach a crosspaths and turn right to climb directly up, eventually swinging left to a clearing marked with a bench and a picnic table. This is a stunning viewpoint, with Porthmadog and the coast just a stone's throw away and the Afon Dwyryd winding its way along the valley floor beneath your feet.

Follow the path behind the bench to loop back to the path you walked up on, and drop back down to the crosspaths,

◀ Llyn Mair

where you keep straight ahead to descend steeply to another forest track. Turn right and then, after a few paces, turn left onto another forest track that runs parallel to the railway line. This drops to cross the railway line at a gate and then continues down to a junction, where you keep right to reach a barrier and a better track on a hairpin bend.

Keep ahead on this track as it becomes concrete and drops to a junction on the shores of Llyn Mair. Turn left to follow the path and eventually veer away from the water to a junction with a forest track. Turn right and follow it into a picnic area. Go through the gate on the left, cross the road into the car park, then keep slightly right to walk between two wooden posts and join a good path that climbs up with a stream to its left.

Follow this up to Tan-y-Bwlch Station and cross the bridge to continue on a footpath out onto a narrow lane. Turn right onto this, then left to drop back down through woodland to the main road and the car park at the start.

Coed Felenrhyd

Distance 6.5km Time 2 hours 30
Terrain good footpaths and forest tracks
with a short section on a road at the
start/finish Map OS Explorer OL18
Access no public transport to the start

This walk starts off by exploring the
Ceunant Llennyrch National Nature
Reserve, before climbing out of the steep-
sided heavily wooded gorge to visit Llyn
Tecwyn Uchaf – a picturesque upland
reservoir flanked by a footpath.

The outward leg climbs steeply through
the woods to the plateau above on a
narrow scenic path that's a real pleasure
to follow. The forest tracks above are
easier going and lead to the lake, which is
a great place for a spot of lunch or a snack.
The return leg wanders back through the
forest, still on good tracks, before
eventually plummeting steeply back
down to the valley floor.

There is limited parking at a lay-by
1.5km southwest of Maentwrog on the
A496, just before the Maentwrog Power
Station building. Turn right out of the
lay-by and continue down the road and
across the bridge. Immediately after this,
turn left onto the obvious waymarked
footpath and enter both Coed Felenrhyd
and the Ceunant Llennyrch National
Nature Reserve.

At a fork, keep right to avoid dropping
to the river and then, at the next junction,
stay left. The steep path leading up to
your right is the return route. Now
continue, always uphill, through the
woods, enjoying great views down the
steep hillside to the valley floor.

After a particularly steep section, you'll

◀ Llyn Tecwyn Uchaf

pass through a gate to join a broad track. Keep ahead on this to pass a cottage on your right and soon after turn sharp right onto another forest track. This then bends left and continues undulating easily through the plantation. As you approach Llyn Tecwyn Uchaf turn right and then go left through a gate to walk alongside the water all the way to the beach at the far end. This section is very lovely with rough, rugged hillsides above and the steel-grey waters down to the left. It's also completely optional so if time is tight, it is easy to leave out.

Retrace your steps to the gate and this time keep straight ahead to follow the forest track back into the plantation. Carry on ahead at a junction with a track on the left and continue for another 500m or so before turning left onto a clearly signed narrow footpath. Follow this steeply downhill and around a few sharp bends to eventually meet your outward path. Turn left to retrace your steps to the lay-by.

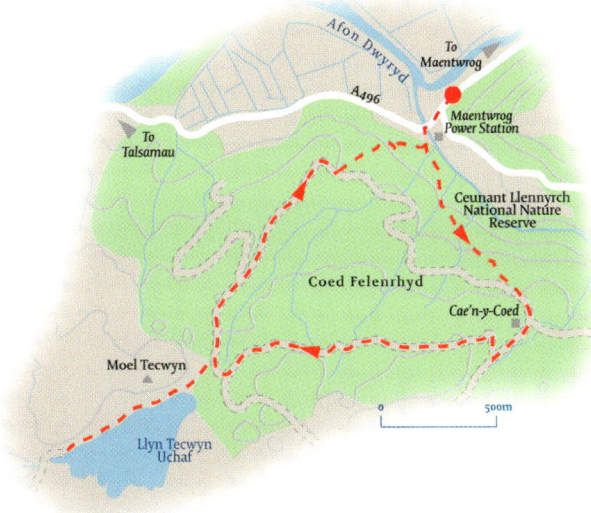

Coed Ganllwyd and Rhaeadr Ddu

Distance 4km **Time** 1 hour 30
Terrain rocky paths (some awkward), grassy tracks, quiet lane; tricky stiles
Map OS Explorer OL18 **Access** buses to Ganllwyd from Bangor, Caernarfon and Dolgellau

Rhaeadr Ddu, or the 'Black Falls' as it translates, is an unexpected delight. While many visitors flock to the Coed y Brenin Visitor Centre some 3.7km to the north on the east side of the Afon Eden, far fewer trek up into the Coed Ganllwyd National Nature Reserve to explore this hidden gem.

The falls themselves are incredibly dramatic, especially in flood and up close, but this whole section of the Afon Gamlan is spectacular and the tumbling cascades make a fine companion to the opening stages of this walk. Later, it leaves the forest and climbs high onto the hillside to visit the remains of the Cefn Coch Gold Mine – an impressive ruin that was still in use in the early 1900s. The views from this section are striking too. The gold mine and Coed Ganllwyd National Nature Reserve are part of the Dolmelynllyn Estate, managed by the National Trust.

Follow the path out of the Dolmelynllyn car park, on the A470 in the centre of Ganllwyd, and cross the road to the lovely corrugated-iron village hall. Go through the walkers' gate and head up the lane, soon climbing steeply with the roaring cascades of the Afon Gamlan to your left. Keep following signs to Rhaeadr Ddu and go straight ahead on a forest track when the road bends sharp right.

Follow this to the falls, where there's a good viewpoint, and then cross the river on the bridge beneath them. Turn right to follow a narrow rocky path up to the falls

Coed Ganllwyd and Rhaeadr Ddu

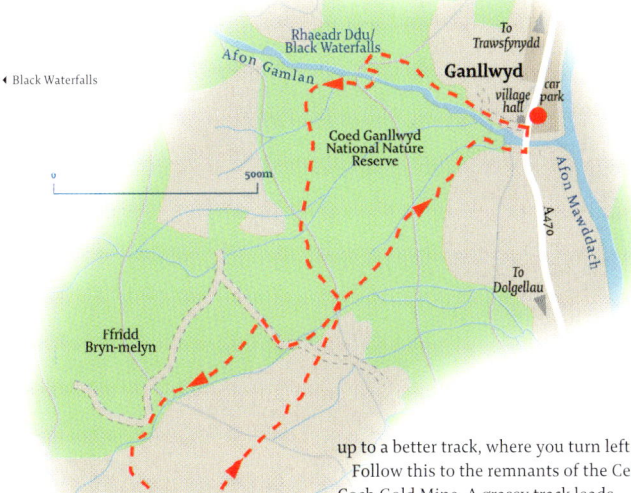

◀ Black Waterfalls

again, and wind your way up above them, where you get great views down over the entire falls. Then continue upwards, all the time following markers, until you eventually reach the top of the forest at a gate. Go through and keep ahead to a wall, where you turn right to a gate on your left that leads onto a footbridge.

Cross, then turn right to walk steeply uphill on a grassy track to join a metalled road. Turn right onto it for a few paces, then at a crossroads turn left onto a forest track. Climb steeply up to a footpath sign on the left and cross a stile and a footbridge to reach a sheep pasture. Turn right to take a rising grassy track up to a better track, where you turn left.

Follow this to the remnants of the Cefn Coch Gold Mine. A grassy track leads uphill with the mine building to your right; you then trend leftwards to enjoy easy walking along an old tramway with great views over the valley below and the hillsides opposite.

At a waymark sign, turn sharp left and walk down to a gate. Go through and continue downhill, crossing a succession of stiles to reach the road again. Cross this and drop to the footbridge you crossed earlier. Go over this and through the gate, then turn right. Now carry straight on, with the wall initially to your right.

Follow this stony track down through the forest, eventually joining another wall on the right and crossing a stile to walk through sheep pasture to a gate that leads onto the A470. Go through, cross the road and turn left to return to the car park.

Coed y Brenin

Distance 4.5km **Time** 1 hour 30
Terrain good paths and forest tracks
Map OS Explorer OL23 **Access** no public transport to the start

Coed y Brenin – the King's Forest – is the perfect name for a majestic woodland. There are many great walks in and around Coed y Brenin but this one stands out, combining woodland with views of one of the area's mightiest rivers, a visit to an impressive waterfall and a chance to learn about the forest's industrial past via the ruins of an old gold mine. It is well-sheltered and on good tracks – ideal if the weather is not so good.

Leave the A470 on the minor road by the village sign at the north end of Ganllwyd and follow it past a couple of car parks to reach Tyddyn Gwladys car park on your right. Go slowly – along the way you are likely to encounter many mountain bikers and to see bike trails diving into the trees. Coed y Brenin was Britain's first purpose-built mountain biking centre and remains a mecca for mountain bikers of all levels, as well as runners and walkers.

A narrow path leads out of the top of the car park and soon joins a broader trail that zigzags down to a bridge. Cross this, stopping to take in the views up and down the Afon Mawddach, and then continue up to join a main forest track on the other side.

Turn left and follow this track easily along, with great views down to the river. The track undulates slightly, but all the time with the river down to the left. You'll see an interpretation sign at the top of the steepest climb – this offers you your first sighting of the old Gwynfynydd gold mine, which closed in 1999. The sign

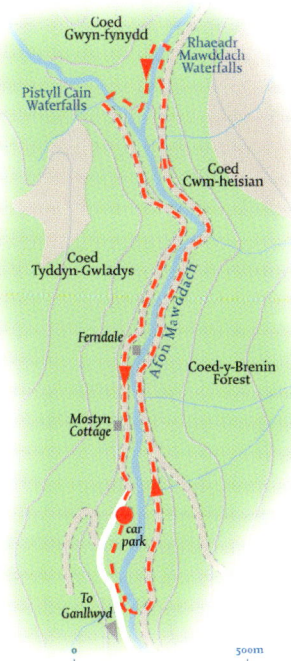

◀ Rhaeadr Mawddach Waterfalls

provides some interesting detail about gold mining in the area.

Continue in the same direction and at a fork bear left to walk steeply downhill to a lovely old stone bridge. This is as far upstream as this route goes, so stop and enjoy the views up towards the source of the Mawddach and then bear left to start walking downstream.

You'll soon arrive at the site of the old gold mine, where there are good views over the river and a large waterfall. It is an excellent spot to stop for a snack. A small hydro-power scheme now utilises the flow of the Afon Mawddach at this point.

Continue downstream, passing or enjoying other viewpoints, before veering around to the right and joining the Afon Gain – a tributary of the Afon Mawddach. Carry on for a few paces to a metal bridge, with magnificent views upstream to a waterfall that plummets into an impressive gorge.

Continue with the thundering Afon Cain to your left until it soon joins with the Afon Mawddach. Keep ahead, now once again with the Afon Mawddach to your left, and pass the remains of the old Tyddyn Gwladys Gunpowder Works. There's a sizeable infrastructure here with buildings, water channels, a tramway and an aqueduct. The works were opened around 1887 with the buildings being taken over by the gold mine by 1893.

Continue to a barrier close to the buildings at Ferndale and keep ahead to pass Mostyn Cottage, where tarmac then leads back to the car park.

Above Barmouth

Distance 7km **Time** 3 hours
Terrain tough walking on tarmac, boggy paths and wooded paths; steep sections
Map OS Explorer OL18 **Access** no public transport to the start, but trains from Machynlleth and Pwllheli and buses from Porthmadog, Dolgellau and Llangollen to Barmouth, 2km from the start

Barmouth is a busy little seaside town at the mouth of the impressive Mawddach Estuary. It is a quintessential coastal town but also makes a great base for outdoor activities, tucked beneath the Rhinogydd Mountains and close to Cadair Idris. This walk is strenuous but well worth the effort with glorious views over the coast, the estuary and the Cadair Idris range across the valley.

Leave the coast road (A496) just 100m east of the iconic single-track railway bridge over the estuary of the Afon Mawddach to head uphill on Panorama Road, eventually reaching the small Panorama Walk parking area. From here, carry on walking up the road, then turn sharp left uphill. The road gives way to a grassy track that winds right, beneath the rock climbing venue of Barmouth Slabs, and on to the farm buildings at Gellfawr.

Turn left and follow the fence down to cross a stream before turning right onto a better path which leads up and around the hillside with great views. This eventually reaches the ruined buildings at Cell-fechan, where you can turn right for an out-and-back detour to the memorial on Craig-y-Gigfran, which

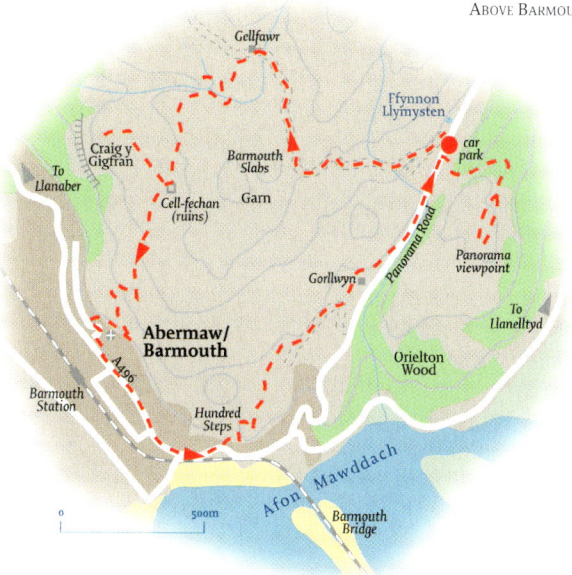

was laid in tribute to the soldiers of the Birmingham District, who died on the first day of the Battle of the Somme.

Retrace your steps to Cell-fechan and continue downhill, all the time with stunning views over the ocean. At a junction, turn sharp right, then zigzag left, then right again to drop to the road near Barmouth. Continue into the town and once on the High Street keep ahead to eventually pass the Last Inn; soon after, at a bend you'll see a set of steep steps leading up to the left.

These are the famous 100 steps and will definitely leave you out of breath by the time you make the top. At a gate, turn right to continue to some houses and then fork left to follow the path around the back of a house, climbing, then dropping to the road. Turn left to walk up the road towards the car park until you reach a gate on your right. This leads onto a short optional detour to the superb Panorama Viewpoint.

After a dip, the path becomes a walled track. Go through a gate and turn right through a second gate on the right. Follow the trail steeply up, keeping left the whole time to eventually spill out onto a rocky ridge with spectacular views over the estuary.

Continue around the ridge before dropping to meet your outward path. Follow this back to the road, where you turn right to finish.

◀ Barmouth Bridge

Precipice Walk

Distance 5.5km **Time** 2 hours
Terrain good well-waymarked paths but very narrow in places with big drops
Map OS Explorer OL23 **Access** infrequent buses from Dolgellau pass the Precipice Walk car park

With the word 'precipice' in the title, you know you're going to experience some exposure on this popular walk. But the good news is, you really don't have to work that hard, with the paths for the most part contouring rather than climbing and dropping.

This is a real gem of a walk, which feels way more 'out there' than it really is and offers stunning views in all directions, from nearby Cadair Idris in the foreground to the imposing Yr Wyddfa massif further north. The Mawddach Estuary takes centre stage; in fact, it's possible to trace its journey almost from source to sea as it rises up on the rounded flanks of Rhobell Fawr to the north of you, and threads its way through the forests of Coed y Brenin, rushing through the valley at your feet before meandering westwards towards the coast at Barmouth.

Start at the car park at the junction with the Hermon road on the main Dolgellau-Llanfachreth road. From the top of the car park, join the Llwybr Cynwch (Precipice Walk) track that leads above the small toilet block and around into forestry. The walk is signed and the paths are clear and easy to follow so navigation should not be an issue.

The path merges with a forest track that comes in from the right, shortly curving right to keep the woods to your right as

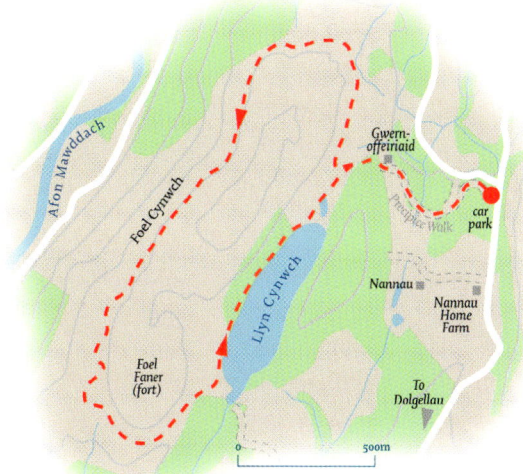

you continue towards a gate and cottage. Here, stay left to climb alongside the wall and then keep right (all the time waymarked) to head beneath tree cover for a few paces to a gate. Go through this, and now on open ground, bear right to follow the path slightly uphill with Llyn Cynwch ahead – you'll pass this on your return journey.

Climb to a gateway and continue out onto open hillside, where the path narrows and the exposed section begins. The views also start to open up for the first time. Your navigation work is now over and all you need to do is stay with the path as it contours around the hill, heading first west, and then south, with views towards Dolgellau, Cadair Idris and, of course, the Mawddach Estuary.

You'll pass through a couple of gates but stay with the obvious path and then eventually, as it reaches its furthest southwest point, you'll see a bench straight ahead – a fine spot for a snack or lunch, or just to take in the views.

Return to the path and continue through a gate in a wall, across a pasture and then around the hillside once more before dropping to the shores of Llyn Cynwch. There are paths running along both sides of the lake but the one along the western bank is narrower and more in keeping with the general nature of the walk. Follow the lake shore to the far end where you'll rejoin the path you walked in on. Keep ahead to enter the small copse again and then simply retrace your steps to the car park.

◂ Looking down over the Afon Mawddach

Llynnau Cregennen

Distance 9km **Time** 2 hours 30
Terrain good paths that can get muddy and narrow lanes; optional scramble
Map OS Explorer OL23 **Access** no public transport to the start

The mini-mountain of Pared y Cefn hir stands just 383m above sea level yet is one of the most shapely and dramatic peaks in Eryri. The mountain would be impressive enough on its own, but the fact that it towers above two stunning mountain tarns and has great views over both the coast and the much loftier Cadair Idris range makes it an even more rewarding place to walk.

A word of warning: the true traverse of the summit involves a few short sections of scrambling where hands will definitely be needed as well as feet. The main walk described here flanks the peak to the east and is considerably easier.

The lakes car park road links the A493 just north of Arthog with the old Dolgellau mountain road and is signed for Llynnau Cregennen at both ends. Walk back out of the car park, turn left onto the road and then go right onto a footpath just beyond a gate. Follow it over a ladder stile and then, where the path forks, head

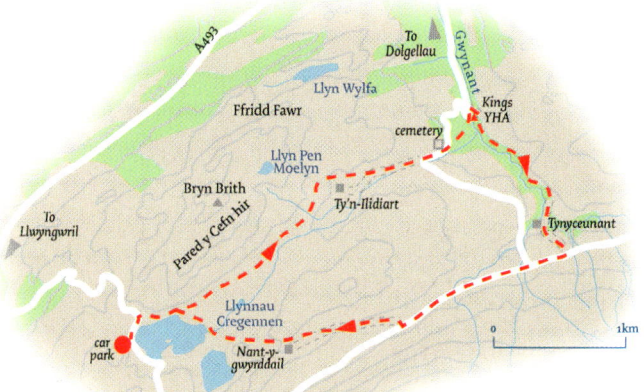

right towards the lake (scramblers bear left here and tackle the summit and ridge directly). The path now drops to the lake shore and follows it for a while before continuing easily along the foot of the steep ground, eventually reaching a gate. (Scramblers will rejoin this flanking path before it reaches the gate.)

Carry on across the field beyond to a gap in a wall and stay ahead to join a track with a stream down to the right. Continue out onto a road and keep straight ahead, still with the stream to your right, until you reach an atmospheric ruin and a cemetery on your left. Stay straight ahead as the road bends left to follow an obvious but often muddy path down through woodland to join the road at the bottom. Turn right onto this and drop to a junction where you turn sharp right with Kings YHA on your right. Walk up past the hostel and then turn right onto a track that leads through a camping field and onto a footpath.

Follow this beautiful wooded walkway uphill, enjoying a river down to your right for the most part. Eventually, this leads to farm buildings where you follow the drive up to the road. Turn right for some easy tarmac walking, passing a junction on the right after 300m and then another farm track on the right after a further 500m.

Some 400m after this track, you meet another track on the right – take this to climb steeply to farm buildings. Keep these to your left and follow waymarks away, eventually dropping to flat ground. Keep ahead to Llynnau Cregennan and continue in the same direction, crossing a stile, to rejoin your outward path. Turn left to retrace your steps to the car park.

Cadair Idris

Distance 9km **Time** 4 hours
Terrain mainly clear paths, rocky in places, that climb and descend a high mountain
Map OS Explorer OL23 **Access** no public transport to the start

Cadair Idris is a big mountain in every sense of the word. It towers high above Dolgellau and the surrounding countryside with a distinctive profile that's easily identified from miles away. It's also quite unique, having steep-sided cirques, or cwms as they are known in Wales, to both the north and south of the summit.

This walk explores the mountain from the north, where it makes a bold approach via two stunning mountain lakes – Llyn Gafr and Llyn y Gadair. The final slopes are steep but the summit is one of the best viewpoints in Wales. The descent is slightly less challenging but equally as enthralling, especially if combined with an optional crossing of the nearby summit of Cyfrwy.

Start at the Ty-nant car park at the foot of the Pony Path on the old Dolgellau mountain road, about 4km west of Dolgellau. Walk back out of the car park, turn left and follow the road until you are parallel with Llyn Gwernan, then look out for a footpath on the right – this is the Fox's Path. Follow the path across rolling ground to a stile which leads out onto open moorland. Keep straight ahead, fording a couple of small brooks before

reaching another stile. Keep ahead again here and climb up to the outflow of the lovely Llyn Gafr (Lake of the Goat) – a fine viewpoint.

From here, keep straight ahead to climb steeply up to Llyn y Gadair – a stunning mountain lake, guarded on three sides by towering rock walls. To the right is the jagged ridge of the Cyfrwy Arête. The path continues around the eastern shores of Llyn y Gadair and brings you to a steep slope that leads to the summit. Push on and you'll eventually emerge onto the summit plateau. Follow the faint path towards the rock-crowned summit, which has a small shelter next to it. On a clear day you should be able to make out pretty much the whole of Eryri to the north, as well as the main peaks of the Brecon Beacons many miles to the south.

The descent follows the Pony Path – probably the mountain's most popular route. This initially hugs the northern escarpment but eventually breaks away to avoid the climb up to the outlying top of Cyfrwy. If you've energy to spare, bear right and walk over this top, which offers terrific views down over Llyn y Gadair and your ascent route. From here, continue south to rejoin the Pony Path – now marked with cairns every few metres – and follow it easily down into the broad saddle that separates the main mountain from the outlying top of Carnedd Lŵyd.

The track swings right here and soon becomes much steeper as it drops onto the huge plateau below. Stay with the path as it levels and crosses easier ground to a gate. Now continue, steeply once more, until you reach the road. Turn right to finish.

◀ Cadair Idris and Llyn y Gadair

Nant Gwernol

Distance 7km Time 2 hours 30
Terrain clear paths, though some muddy, and a short section on a quiet lane
Map OS Explorer OL23 Access buses to Abergynolwyn from Tywyn, Dolgellau and Machynlleth

The rushing Nant Gwernol carves a deep defile in the northern flanks of the Tarrenau – Eryri's most southerly mountain range. This walk follows the tumbling stream, offering grandstand views of a succession of waterfalls before climbing high into the hills to visit the ruins of the Bryn Eglwys Slate Quarry – a substantial operation in its day with much still to see. The walk starts in the pretty little quarrying village of Abergynolwyn, well worth a visit in its own right.

From the centre of Abergynolwyn, walk up the narrow lane with the community centre to your right and climb steeply to a waymarked footpath on the right. Take this and follow it into the cover of trees, where you first see the rushing Nant Gwernol down below. The path cuts a lovely line above the stream, passing a number of small cascades, some with deep pools below, before reaching a footbridge that spans the river.

Cross this and climb steeply up the other side to Nant Gwernol Station – the eastern terminus of the Talyllyn Railway. Turn sharp left here to continue upwards to join a more level track. Keep straight ahead now to walk easily through the woods, with the river way down to your left, until you reach another footbridge.

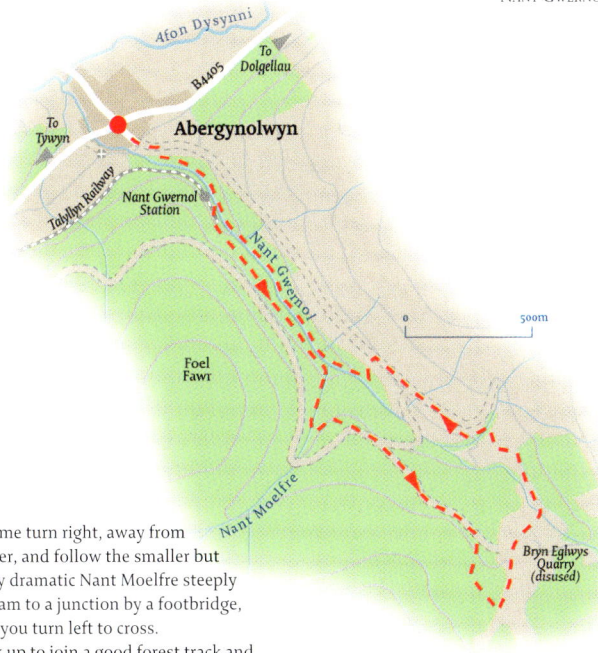

This time turn right, away from the river, and follow the smaller but equally dramatic Nant Moelfre steeply upstream to a junction by a footbridge, where you turn left to cross.

Walk up to join a good forest track and follow this left, keeping right at a fork after a few paces. Continue now until you reach a waymark post on the left, where you turn right to climb steeply up a rough and often wet path. Follow this up and around to the left where it contours through the woods, then drops towards the Bryn Eglwys Quarry. As well as the fascinating ruins, there's an interesting information board that shows the quarry as it would have been.

Continue down to a large flat clearing and keep straight ahead, now on a grassy track that leads over a footbridge. Stay with this track, which can be muddy, as it curves leftwards to start heading back down the valley. Carry on to a gate and go through this to pass a waterfall, then continue across sheep pasture to reach a gate and a waymarked footpath.

Go through the gate and drop steeply down zigzags to rejoin the Nant Gwernol – now on your left. Turn right to walk downstream and enjoy another series of spectacular cascades before it eventually takes you back to the footbridge you crossed earlier. Keep straight ahead to retrace your steps down to Abergynolwyn.

◂ Bryn Eglwys Quarry ruin

Llyn Barfog

Distance 4.5km **Time** 2 hours
Terrain clear well-marked paths and tracks with one slightly vague section
Map OS Explorer OL23 **Access** no public transport to the start

Although quite short, this is a wonderful walk with real variety. It starts with an easy saunter through farm buildings, followed by a tough climb. But once up, that's pretty much all the ascent for the whole walk and the views over the Afon Dyfi and Cardigan Bay more than compensate for the hard work. Later, there are views north to the Tarren Hills – Eryri's southernmost mountain range. Then, of course, there's Llyn Barfog itself – a beautiful spot set amidst wild scenery.

Start at the Llyn Barfog (Bearded Lake) car park in Cwm Maethlon, 8km east of Tywyn on the Cwm Maethlon Road. Leave the car park by a gate at its far end and turn left onto the drive. Pass a cottage and a farmyard and then walk up through another farmyard.

Immediately after leaving the farmyard by a gate, turn right and brace yourself for a steep clamber up onto the ridge above. At the top, you'll pass a cottage where a gate leads onto another track. Thankfully, the climbing is over now, so turn left and enjoy some easy walking with huge views down over your right shoulder to the Afon Dyfi.

Continue easily, shortly with a dry-stone wall to your right. You soon pass

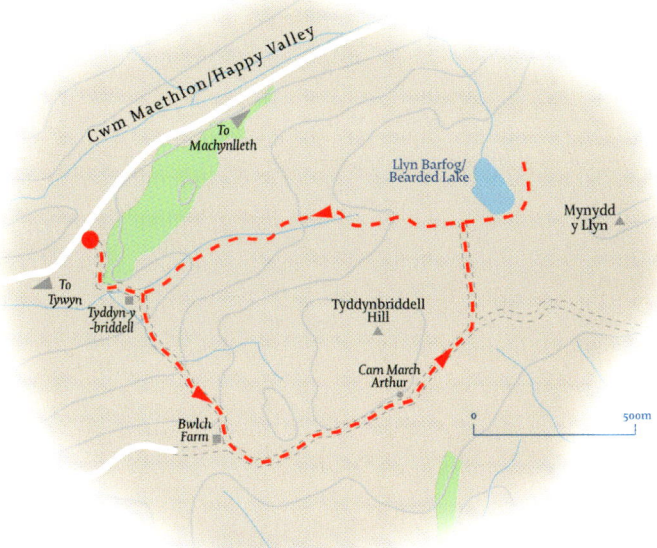

Carn March Arthur – where an indentation in the rock is said to be a hoofprint from King Arthur's horse. Eventually, you pass through a gate and come to a fork in the track. Turn left here onto a grassy path that leads over the crest of the ridge before dropping steeply down towards Llyn Barfog. Near the bottom, you'll meet another path. Turn right onto this to walk past the head of the lake, go through a gate and continue, gradually trending leftwards for a steep climb on a faint path up to a heathery summit, topped with an impressive cairn.

Return through the gate and to the point where you joined the lakeside path earlier. This time, keep straight ahead to continue down into Cwm Maethlon, or Happy Valley as it's also known. Pass through a gate close to a spectacular crag and walk downhill on a good farm track to soon reach the gate you came through earlier at the entrance to the farmyard. Retrace your earlier footsteps to the start.

◄ Llyn Barfog

Wales is proud of its Coast Path and no visit to North Wales is complete without taking in the sea air.

Although it lies outside the national park, the Llŷn Peninsula has some spectacular mountainous walks. The Yr Eifl range offers both the finest and the highest views out over the sea while shorter routes here visit greened-over quarries and tramways, as well as a secluded and very wild beach. Criccieth represents the grander side of the peninsula with a grand castle, an elegant promenade and the lovely Afon Dwyfor. Further north, walks around Ynys Môn (Anglesey) take in Holyhead Mountain, the highest point on Holy Island, a beautiful section of the Anglesey Coast Path from Porth Swtan and magical Ynys Llanddwyn, an island dotted with monuments.

The routes divert from the coast to explore Aber Falls, one of the highest waterfalls in Wales, and Conwy Mountain, an incredible viewpoint squeezed between the ocean and the towering peaks of the Carneddau range.

It's then back to the coast to finish with an easy but enthralling lap of the Great Orme – an imposing headland that thrusts seaward from the classic Victorian beachside resort of Llandudno.

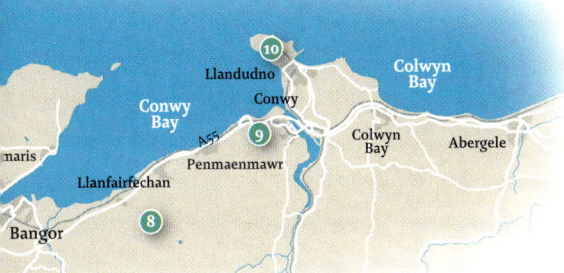

Anglesey, the Llŷn Peninsula and the North Coast

1. Aberdaron and Pen y Cil — 76
Hike around the remote southern tip of the beautiful Llŷn Peninsula

2. Yr Eifl and Tre'r Ceiri hillfort — 78
This tough outing up 'the Rivals' rewards with stunning mountain and coastal views

3. Trefor and Trwyn-y-Tâl — 80
Remember your binoculars for this walk along one of the best stretches of the Llŷn Peninsula coastline

4. Criccieth and the Afon Dwyfor — 82
Follow the shoreline beneath a magnificent headland castle, then dive inland on a varied circuit

5. Traeth Llanddwyn — 84
Stroll along golden sands before heading out to the old lighthouse

6. Holyhead Mountain — 86
Explore dramatic coastal scenery on this walk to the Isle of Anglesey's windblown western tip

7. Porth Swtan — 88
Stretch your legs on a lovely coastal walk with the option of visiting a pair of islands at low tide

8. Aber Falls — 90
Walk through some wild woodland to reach a truly majestic waterfall

9. Conwy Mountain — 92
Enjoy far-reaching views from the top of an easily-reached ridge

10. Great Orme — 94
Leave Llandudno behind for a tour of this limestone headland full of birdlife and historic interest

Aberdaron and Pen y Cil

Distance 12km Time 4 hours
Terrain waymarked coastal path, narrow lanes Map OS Explorer 253 Access regular buses to Aberdaron from Pwllheli

Pen y Cil is on the southernmost tip of the Llŷn Peninsula, which reaches out 48km into the Irish Sea from northwest Wales. With nearby Braich y Pwll marking the peninsula's westernmost point, it's little wonder this walk feels remote.

The village of Aberdaron is one of the remotest settlements on the peninsula too, although it still manages to thrive as a bustling little coastal resort. This walk explores this far-flung tip of the peninsula, starting on one of Aberdaron's lovely beaches and following the dramatic Wales Coast Path outwards before cutting back across farmland to finish.

Start from the National Trust car park at Aberdaron Beach by Porth y Swnt Visitor Centre. Above the shore to the east is Eglwys St Hywyn, a pilgrim church dating back to medieval times, which is well worth a visit.

The Coast Path leaves the car park and heads up onto cliffs above the beach, but if the tide's not too high you can stay on the beach and follow it westwards to its far end where a good path climbs steeply to join the Coast Path a little further on. The coast makes for easy scenic walking until you drop steeply down to the slipway at Porth Meudwy, where pilgrims once made the 3km journey to Ynys Enlli (Bardsey Island), an important religious site since the 6th century.

Clamber steeply away from the inlet and then settle into a relaxed pace again as the path wends its way above the clifftops. Continue above the old harbour wall at Hen Borth and then out onto the headland at Pen y Cil. The path climbs

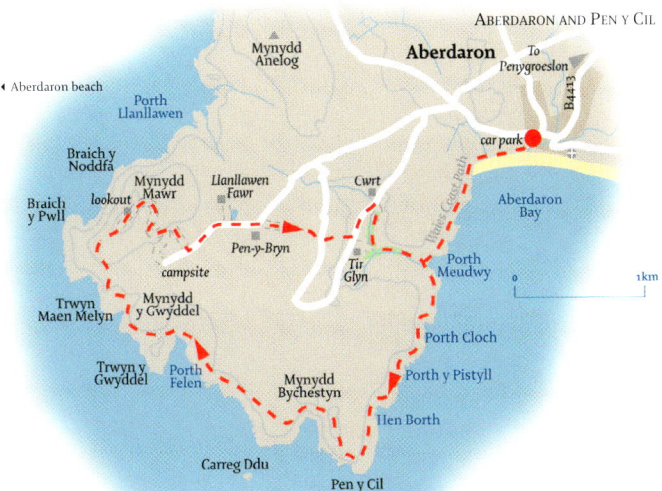

◀ Aberdaron beach

between rocky outcrops with great views over Bardsey Sound before swinging inland, passing a gate on the left to carry on through one ahead and another on the left further inland. Follow the edge of a pasture to a gate onto Mynydd Bychestyn.

Continue straight ahead here towards a marker post and then swing right along a lovely section of path that eventually drops to Porth Felen. Keep ahead to climb steeply into a saddle and take the clear narrow path. This drops into a shallow dell then rises again and contours around the hillside to meet concrete platforms left over from the Second World War buildings, where a set of steps lead directly up to the old coastguard lookout atop Mynydd Mawr.

Follow the drive down around a right and then a left bend. As it bends right again, leave the drive and follow a vague path straight ahead. This leads to a gate above a building. Go through the gate and walk down the drive to the road. Turn left and follow the road easily along to a sharp left bend, where you go straight ahead. Pass farm buildings and keep ahead into a field. Carry on ahead, over a stile, onto a hedged path and follow this to the road.

Turn right and then left to follow a raised path to another road before turning left along this for a short distance. The road leads past Cwrt farm, the National Trust's ranger base – once known as Abbots Court, the administrative centre for Bardsey's monastery and its properties. Before you get to the buildings, turn right at a 'Cwrt' sign onto a concrete drive. Follow this to Porth Meudwy where you rejoin the Coast Path. Retrace your steps to Aberdaron.

ANGLESEY, THE LLŶN PENINSULA AND THE NORTH COAST

Yr Eifl and Tre'r Ceiri hillfort

Distance 7km **Time** 3 hours
Terrain a mix of good footpaths and tracks, with a few steep, awkward sections
Map OS Explorer 254 **Access** buses from Pwllheli to Llithfaen, 1km from the start

The jagged peaks of Yr Eifl, also known as 'the Rivals,' dominate the northern coast of the Llŷn Peninsula, and while they would be easily overlooked for the more famous peaks of Eryri just a few miles east, to do so would be to miss out on some of the finest mountain walking in North Wales. This is a challenging walk, despite the modest length, and definitely worth saving for a good day.

The Yr Eifl car park is reached by taking the mountain road north from the crossroads in Llithfaen, signed for Nant Gwrtheyrn, a Welsh language and heritage centre (with café) set in a former quarrying village, which is located just over the hill from the car park.

From the car park, cross the road to join the wide stony track that heads easily uphill, keeping the towering bulk of Yr Eifl to your right. This section provides a great warm-up for things to come with stunning views down over Nant Gwrtheyrn to the sea beyond. In the distance you can clearly see Anglesey, as well as the mountains of Eryri. Ahead is the outline of Garn For adorned with a mast. This small but spectacular mountain is your first objective.

When you reach the saddle between Yr Eifl and Garn For and see the path to Yr Eifl waymarked to the right, turn left onto a clear track and follow it up to the telecoms tower. Carry on following the vague steps which wind through the scree to eventually spill you out onto soft ground near the summit with most of the coast peninsula now stretching out below.

Retrace your steps down to the saddle and this time take the steep path up

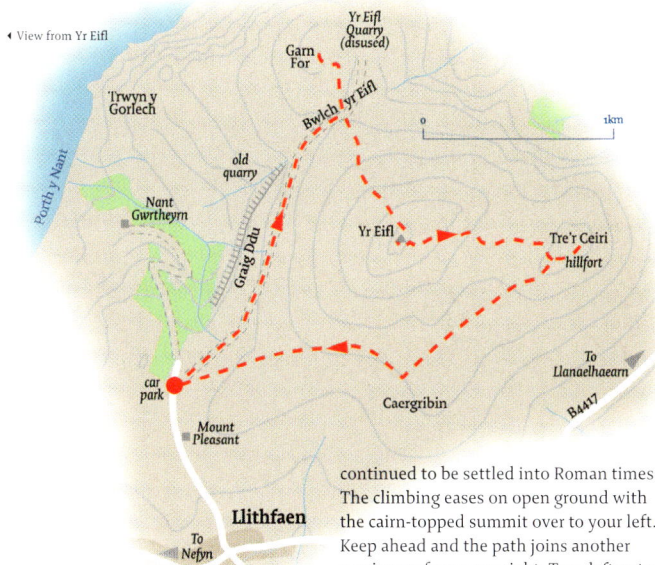

◀ View from Yr Eifl

towards Yr Eifl. After a short sharp climb, you reach the summit plateau, with the trig point and a shelter over to your right and a clear view of the fortifications on Tre'r Ceiri, the second highest peak of the range and your next challenge.

Drop down the narrow path that leads east towards the hillfort of Tre'r Ceiri, which means 'Town of the Giants', and wind your way steeply down into a boggy col between the two peaks. Keep ahead to soon climb again, this time up through the amazingly intact walls of the hillfort, some of which are 4m high. Described as 'one of the most spectacular ancient monuments in Wales', the Iron Age fort continued to be settled into Roman times. The climbing eases on open ground with the cairn-topped summit over to your left. Keep ahead and the path joins another coming up from your right. Turn left onto this and gradually trend leftwards to follow the wall up to the top.

To descend, retrace your steps to where the paths meet, then keep straight ahead to drop down through another gateway in the walls to the heathery plateau below. A good path leads through this to a gate, where you'll see a nature reserve interpretation board.

Keep ahead to follow the path across easy, relatively flat ground to another gate where you bear slightly right to climb a little before swinging left again, continuing on easier graded ground. Stay with this now, keeping straight ahead at a crossroads of tracks, and you'll eventually see the car park below you.

ANGLESEY, the LLŶN PENINSULA and the NORTH COAST

Trefor and Trwyn-y-Tâl

Distance 4km **Time** 1 hour 30
Terrain coastal path, close to cliff edges in places, farm tracks and small roads through Trefor village **Map** OS Explorer 254
Access bus to Trefor from Caernarfon and Pwllheli

The section of Coast Path that leads west over Trwyn-y-Tâl from Trefor is probably the finest stretch of path on the northern side of the Llŷn Peninsula, with easy relatively level walking and great views.

You'll pass the remnants of slate quarries and look out over the small islands of Ynys Bâch and Ynys Fawr and the seabird colony on the Trefor Sea Stack. This is also a great place to see choughs – a small corvid with a bright red beak and legs and a distinctive call. The Coast Path section of the walk ends at a remote beach and the return leg crosses sheep pasture and winds through the narrow streets of Trefor, although it's always possible to retrace your steps if you'd prefer to be by the coast.

Start from the car park at Traeth Trefor, accessed via the minor road signed for the beach by the bus stop at the east end of Trefor. Walk back out of the car park and down to the beach where you need to turn left. You can walk along the beach at this point or along the road that runs behind it. Either way, at the far end, you'll pass through a gate by the harbour wall. Continue above the next beach and across a footbridge to continue through a kissing gate at the entrance to the National Trust land at Morfa.

Climb steeply up onto the Wales Coast Path, which you now follow straight

◀ Looking towards Trwyn y Gorlech

ahead through the remnants of the Morfa slate quarries with steep cliffs to your right. Follow marker posts along this wonderful section of the Coast Path and you'll pass the small island of Ynys Bâch and Trefor Sea Stacks, usually covered with seabirds.

Keep ahead until you reach a pair of gates in front of you; go through the right-hand gate to drop down a narrow path towards an obvious dip. Steps lead down to the beach here – a lovely remote spot for a little detour. Carry on ahead to leave the Coast Path and go through a gate to continue uphill, with a cottage over to your right.

Go through two more gates into sheep pasture and stay on the broad track through two fields to a gate that leads between buildings. Keep ahead now to soon enter the village, with terraced houses on both sides. Continue to the end of the road and turn left to pass the village shop. Follow this road as it weaves around to eventually return to the triangular road junction and bus stop.

Keep left onto Beach Road to walk between houses and around a sharp left-hand bend. Now drop down the hill until you reach the beach and car park.

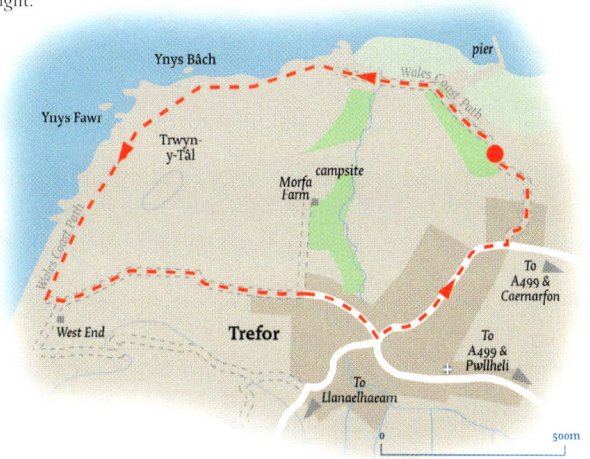

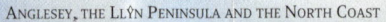

Criccieth and the Afon Dwyfor

Distance 10km **Time** 3 hours
Terrain a mix of good footpaths with short sections on tarmac
Map OS Explorer 254 **Access** Criccieth is well served by trains and buses

The seaside town of Criccieth sits on the southeast corner of the Llŷn Peninsula. It's a bustling little place, dominated by the ruins of an imposing castle, which is where this walk starts. Like most of the rivers in these parts, the Afon Dwyfor rises up in the high mountains of Eryri, before making the short but turbulent journey to the sea just west of the town.

This walk follows the coast from Criccieth as far as the point where the Dwyfor empties into the sea, before returning along a beautiful wooded path that follows its banks. Along the way, it passes the grave of David Lloyd George, the last Liberal Party prime minister of the United Kingdom (1916-1922) who was known for his social-reform policies and for negotiating the establishment of the Irish Free State. The final leg leads easily across fields back to the town.

Parking can be found along the esplanade to the east of the castle and at the Traeth Criccieth car park. With Castell Cricieth up to your left, continue onto the seafront and past a row of colourful houses. As the promenade ends, keep straight ahead to join the Coast Path, with great views both along the coast and back over the Rhinogydd Mountains. After well over 2km, you are ushered inland by the mouth of the Afon Dwyfor.

Follow the river easily upstream and over a boardwalk section, continuing to a gate. Go through and then turn right to follow the field edge up over the railway

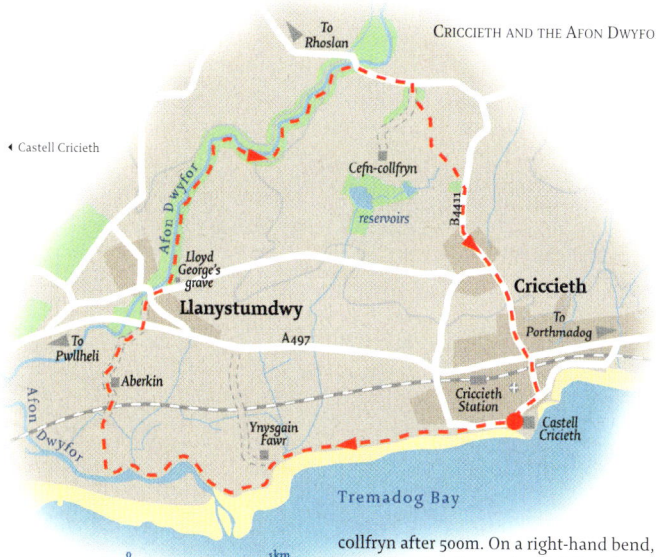

line, and on to the farmyard at Aberkin. Keep straight ahead through the farm and continue along the drive to the A497.

Go straight across and join a footpath that continues past houses and delivers you onto the road at Llanystumdwy. Turn left onto the road and then right before the bridge, signed for Lloyd George's grave. Turn left onto a footpath and then follow this, with the lovely Afon Dwyfor on your left, to pass the grave before continuing easily upstream. In spring, this section is awash with bluebells.

The next few miles simply follow the river, always keeping it to your left. Ignore paths leading right until you eventually emerge on the B4411. Turn right onto this, then turn right onto the drive for Cefn-collfryn after 500m. On a right-hand bend, bear left onto a footpath and follow this out into pasture. Keep the fence on your left to cross a stile in a field corner, now continuing with the fence to your right. After another stile, head diagonally left to another and cross a drive and a further stile to carry on in the same direction to rejoin the B4411.

Turn right onto this and follow it easily back into town, where you keep straight ahead to the spectacular headland castle. First built in the 13th century by Llywelyn the Great and extended by Llywelyn the Last, and by Edward I after the garrison was lost to the English, Castell Criccieth fell out of use after being razed, most probably in 1404 by Owain Glyndwr. The subsequent ruin was the subject of several sketches by J M W Turner between 1798 and 1835 and is well worth a visit.

Traeth Llanddwyn

Distance **6.5km** Time **2 hours 30**
Terrain **sandy paths and grassy tracks with a long walk along a sandy beach; check tide times before setting out**
Map **OS Explorer 254** Access **no public transport to the start**

The southwestern corner of Anglesey is defined by the stunning golden sands of Traeth Llanddwyn, or Newborough Sands, backed by the magnificent Corsican pines of Newborough Forest and bordered to the northwest by the wonderfully atmospheric peninsula of Llanddwyn Island.

Whether it's an island or a peninsula is decided by the time of day, with the waters cutting off access altogether at high tide. Highlights include an old lighthouse, the remains of a church and two impressive crosses. There are also many opportunities to drop off the path and explore sheltered, hidden coves.

Newborough Forest itself has plenty to keep all the family active, with a trim trail, orienteering courses, and running, riding, cycling and walking trails. Start at the Ynys Llanddwyn beach car park at the edge of the forest. From here, go through the gap in the sand dunes and walk out onto the beach. You will now see Ynys Llanddwyn at the other end of the beach to your right and all you need to do is stroll along the sands until you reach the rocky outcrops at its foot. Continue to the furthest set of rocks, which line up with a set of steps leading up onto the island.

TRAETH LLANDDWYN

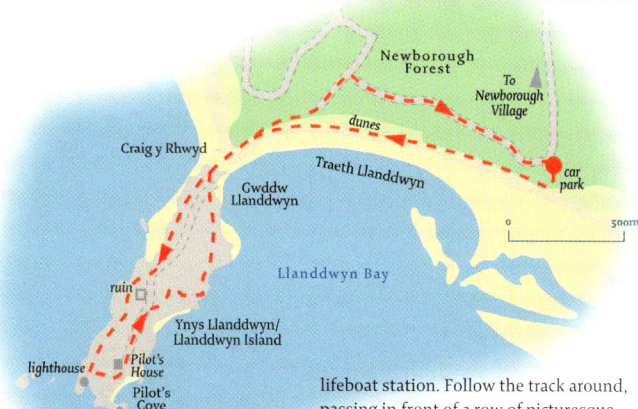

Head up the steps and follow the path easily along with the sea to your right. This is a lovely section with easy ground underfoot and great sea views. Pass above the beautiful golden sands of West Beach and meet the main track. Keep right so you are still hugging the coast, and pass the ruins of Eglwys Santes Dwynwen down to your left. Shortly beyond here, you'll reach St Dwynwen's Cross. Keep straight ahead to the tip of the island and the spectacularly positioned Goleudy Twr Mawr, or Twr Mawr Lighthouse, which was built in 1873 and marks the western entrance to the Menai Strait. The tower is well worth climbing.

Return to the main island and cross to the east side of the peninsula. If you feel like exploring further, there's Goleudy Twr Bach (Small Tower) and the old lifeboat station. Follow the track around, passing in front of a row of picturesque cottages used by pilots who would board ships to help captains navigate the Menai Strait in the 19th century. In front is a large signal cannon, which was used to summon villagers from Newborough to help man the lifeboat. Beyond this is one of the island's most photogenic coves.

The route continues ahead to the Celtic cross where you leave the main path to follow a lesser path to the right that undulates along the east coast, passing above numerous beaches, most of which are accessible and usually quite sheltered.

On reaching the main beach, you can either retrace your steps along the sand or follow easy paths back through the fantastic Corsican pine forest that rises above the dunes. To do this, head up the top of the beach and turn back towards the car park. Then fork left onto a clear sandy track that leads to a forest road; follow this into the trees for 200m, then turn right onto a track that leads back to the main car park.

◀ Twr Mawr Lighthouse

Holyhead Mountain

Distance 8km **Time** 2 hours 30
Terrain confusing paths in places; steep sections, some near cliff edges
Map OS Explorer 262 **Access** no public transport to the start

Often described as the Land's End of Wales, Holyhead Mountain and the towering twin-pronged promontories of South Stack and North Stack form the western tip of Holy Island, itself the western tip of the Isle of Anglesey.

The vertiginous cliffs, heathery heathland and crashing surf combine to produce some of the most dramatic coastal scenery found anywhere in the area and it's a superb place for a walk, especially in the evening when the sun sets over the two picturesque lighthouses that bookend the bay.

Start at the Ellin's Tower RSPB car park beside Plas Nico on the South Stack Road, 300m before the Ynys Lawd Visitor Centre. Take the narrow path that leads out of the bottom corner of the car park and follow it towards the sea. You soon meet the Wales Coast Path, which you'll now be on for around half of this walk. Turn right onto the path and enjoy easy walking along the clifftops, with great views over the ocean and ahead towards South Stack Lighthouse. Continue to Ellin's Tower, a white castellated folly that was built in the 19th century and later served as a watchtower during both World Wars. It is now owned by the RSPB.

Follow the path away from the tower and climb steeply to join a road. Turn left and continue the short distance to the end of this. You are now directly above the lighthouse – an optional though strenuous detour. Alternatively, turn right onto the waymarked Coast Path and follow it to a fenced-off enclosure around

◀ Above Gogarth Bay

a radio mast. Turn right to drop to a broad path and go left on this to follow it up onto the lower slopes of Holyhead Mountain.

Stay on the Coast Path, ignoring a right turn to the summit and then a left that heads back towards the clifftops. Climb steeply, all the time following Coast Path markers, cross a flatter area, then climb again over a small hilltop littered with ruined buildings. Drop steeply towards North Stack to approach the buildings on Ynys Arw – once a fog warning station. The small building is known as the Trinity House Magazine and was used to store the ammunition for the warning cannon.

The path now leads right, away from the main track, and climbs steadily for a while before levelling with great views over the harbour at Holyhead. Before you start to drop again, at a post marked SH220 386, turn right onto a narrow path and leave the Coast Path behind. Climb into an obvious dip in the ridge above and turn left onto a good track for a few paces.

Now turn sharp right to climb steeply towards Holyhead Mountain again. Join a good path and go left to follow red arrow signs around the hillside, eventually dropping steeply to walk between walls. Turn right onto another walled track and follow this around the hills, staying with the red arrows the whole time.

You're soon directed right up towards and then beneath the white Holyhead Mountain crags, before turning left onto a major track. Continue until another red arrow directs you left downhill, and keep straight ahead at a junction to meet a lane. Follow the lane back to the road above Ellin's Tower. Turn left to finish.

Anglesey, the Llŷn Peninsula and the North Coast

Porth Swtan

Distance 8km **Time** 3 hours
Terrain a mix of clear coastal path, field paths, farm tracks and a quiet lane
Map OS Explorer 262 **Access** buses from Holyhead, Llanrhyddlad, Amlwch and Llangefni to Rhydwyn, a 2km walk from Porth Swtan

This walk explores a lovely section of the Anglesey Coast Path, taking in some stunning scenery and visiting a remote beach where it's possible at low tide to explore the offshore islands of Ynys Fydlyn.

It's a great section of path to spot wildlife, with seals, porpoises and dolphins all regularly seen, as well as choughs that while nationally rare are common here. The magnificent sands of Porth Swtan provide a fitting finale.

Porth Swtan is named after the River Swtan, a small stream that empties into the sea below Church Bay, and it may refer to the swtan or 'sea white' fish.

The English name, Church Bay, was commonly used by sailors in the 19th century, as the church forming a visible landmark from the sea. Although the English name refers only to the larger bay, it has sadly resulted in the names of many of the smaller coves that make up the bay falling out of use.

Start at the car park near the bottom of the road in Porth Swtan. Turn right out of the car park and after a short distance take a narrow signposted path on the left. After rejoining the road, continue uphill towards the spire of St Rhuddlad's Church and go left along the narrow lane.

As the lane bends, take the path to the right and just before you meet the lane again, go right and cross the stiles,

◂ Ynys y Fydlyn

eventually going around a house to meet a rough track. Continue ahead on this, passing through two gates to join a lane by Orsedd Goch Farm. Bear left onto the lane and follow it for 1km to the National Trust car park at Mynachdy.

Turn left into the car park and go through a gate onto a grassy track that leads alongside a fence, then a forest, until it eventually drops to the beach by Ynys y Fydlyn. If the tide's low enough, it is possible to scramble onto the two islands. To continue, rejoin the Coast Path and follow this around, climbing and dropping many times and skirting around some steep-sided inlets. You're eventually funnelled through a gate above Porth Swtan where you'll soon rejoin your outward route. Now simply retrace your footsteps to the car park.

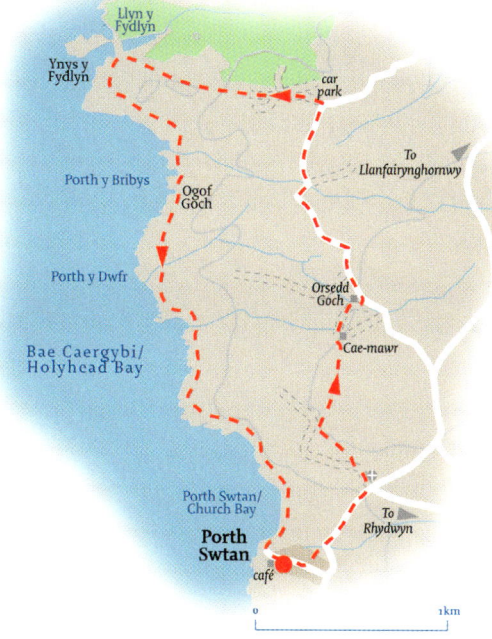

Aber Falls

Distance 6.5km **Time** 2 hours 30
Terrain mainly good footpaths with a short section on a quiet road
Map OS Explorer OL17 **Access** buses from Bangor, Llandudno and Llanfairfechan to Abergwyngregyn, 1.6km from the start

The Carneddau – the northernmost mountain range in Wales – is renowned for its high rugged terrain and uncompromising nature. But many of the massif's highlights are found on the lower slopes and foothills, none more dramatic than Aber Falls, one of the highest waterfalls in Wales and the focal point of this spectacular circular walk.

The outward leg showcases the steep northern slopes of Bera Mawr, down which the Afon Goch tumbles, while the return journey offers huge views over the Menai Strait to the Isle of Anglesey.

To reach the start, turn off the A55 between Bangor and Llanfairfechan at Junction 13, signed for Abergwyngregyn. Once off the A55, there are parking spaces and a bus stop along the road to the left. However, if you arrive early enough or out of season, it is possible to park at the small Coedydd Aber National Nature Reserve car park, 1.6km down the road heading south from Abergwyngregyn – follow the signs for Aber Falls as soon as you leave the A55.

From the car park, ignore the Bont Newydd to the left, and go through the gate at the far end into the nature reserve. Follow the clear path easily along the west bank of the river, then drop to cross it by a bridge. Turn right onto a track and continue easily with the river now to your right. After 500m, at a fork, stay low (right) and continue to the visitor centre.

ABER FALLS

◀ Aber Falls

The visitor centre makes use of an old *hendre*, or summer dwelling, and houses an interesting museum detailing the formation of the valley itself, as well as the area's human history. From here, continue up the valley, eventually going through a gate and arriving at the falls.

The size of Rhaedr-fawr, the Great Falls, is impressive and even more so after heavy rain. It's possible to get a good view from the end of the path on this side but you can get a lot closer on the other side of the river.

Drop down to cross the bridge and then climb back up to the foot of the falls on the western side. From here, head along the obvious path that leads away from the falls, with steep slopes up to your left. Carry on around the head of the valley, crossing a few streams, until the narrow path becomes a broader track that climbs steeply onto the hillside above.

Stay with this for over 1km, then bear right at a fork to pass the top of a wood. Pass through a gate and keep ahead to another. The path starts to drop steeply here to a junction, where you turn right. Cross the hillside on a narrow path and then continue steeply down to a gate that leads out onto the lane at the bottom. Turn right and follow it easily back up to the car park or left for the bus and village. Whisky lovers may be interested in the Aber Falls Distillery where you can sample its single malt Welsh whisky on a tour or visit the café. It is located on the north side of the A55 off Station Road.

ANGLESEY, THE LLŶN PENINSULA AND THE NORTH COAST

Conwy Mountain

Distance 7.5km **Time** 3 hours
Terrain a mix of good footpaths and tracks, with a few steep, awkward sections
Map OS Explorer OL17 **Access** Conwy is well served by buses and trains; Conwy Railway Station is 1km from the start

Conwy Mountain is an amazing place to walk. To the north, the North Wales coast stretches towards the Wirral Peninsula and Merseyside, and to the south are the high peaks of Eryri.

This tiny cluster of modest hills form the northernmost tip of the mighty Carneddau massif, Eryri's northernmost mountain range. It's a position that has been valued through the ages and, as a result, is dotted with ancient landmarks, including standing stones and imposing Iron Age forts. This isn't a long walk, but it's a hilly one, and navigation can be confusing with so many paths to choose from. Save it for a good day and allow plenty of time to enjoy the airy position and the splendid views.

Start at the parking bay on single-track Mountain Road. Following the signs, walk uphill from here and take the footpath on the right after a few paces. Go steeply uphill, at this stage following both the Cambrian Way and the North Wales Path. The going eases and you'll see a crag ahead of you. Follow the path above this and continue easily on a clear grassy path that follows the ridgetop with sweeping views over the coast.

The next steep section takes you up to Castell Caer Seion, an impressive Iron Age hillfort that dates back to around 500BC. The impressively-situated stronghold is

◂ Conwy from Conwy Mountain

unusual as it comprises a smaller, newer fort inside the original larger one. There's an interpretation board near the entrance.

Continue along the ridgetop through the remnants of the fort and then drop steeply, keeping right on the clearest of two paths. This leads easily down into a broad saddle, where you keep ahead to a junction of paths marked with a bench. Here, veer right to climb steeply up towards the summit of Penmaen-bach. The path levels briefly and then drops slightly, shadowing a stone wall before steepening and continuing to the summit.

To descend from here, turn sharp left, back on yourself, and locate a narrow path that leads above the steepest group. Stay with the path and it will eventually drop you to a corner of a wall which you climb steeply alongside. Keep ahead and at the end of the wall, follow the narrow path slightly left to descend steeply to a junction of tracks.

Keep straight ahead here for a few paces and then, at the next junction, turn left to follow another clear track down towards the wall that marks the edge of the open ground. Keeping this to your right, follow the broad, clear path as it undulates a few times before dropping steadily for nearly 2km. Go through a gate onto a track and then follow this all the way back down to the parking bay.

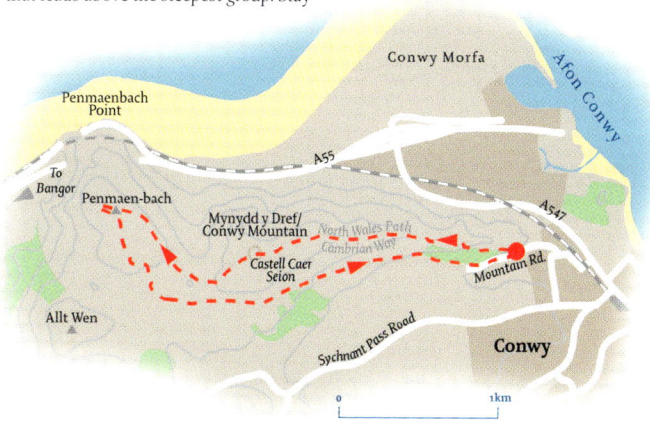

Great Orme

Distance 5.5km **Time** 2 hours
Terrain good footpaths and grassy tracks with a couple of short sections on a quiet, slow tarmac road **Map** OS Explorer OL17
Access buses to the Great Orme summit from Llandudno which is well served by trains and buses

The spectacular limestone headland of the Great Orme is a true highlight of the North Wales coast, jutting defiantly out into the windswept waters of the Irish Sea and rising to more than 200m at its highest point.

On the summit it feels more like a mini-mountain and offers magnificent views in all directions. This walk loops around the upper reaches of the headland, taking in the diminutive St Tudno's Church and passing close to the copper mines. The mines, which date back to the Bronze Age and represent a significant archaeological discovery, were only uncovered in the 1980s and are well worth visiting (seasonal opening). Choose a good day to enjoy views back over Conwy Bay to the mountains of Eryri.

The walk starts in the small parking bay next to St Tudno's Church. This is the lowest point on the walk and, therefore, the easiest place to get to by car. The walk can also be started from the summit. From St Tudno's, walk up the road and around a sharp right-hand bend. Opposite an arched cemetery entrance, go left on a footpath. Follow this up for 500m, then at farm buildings deflect slightly left. Continue out onto open heathland for around 50m, then turn right onto a narrow path through the gorse to reach a crosspaths. Turn right to continue easily across the heathland with great views.

◀ Great Orme headland

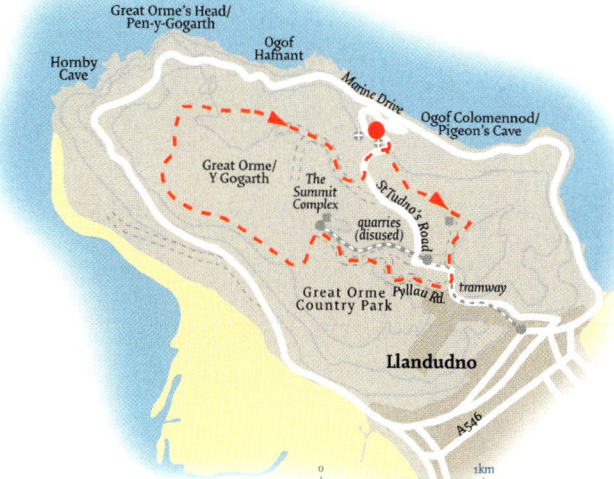

Drop onto a gravel track and turn left to the railway track and road. Keep straight ahead down the road, then take the first right turn onto St Beuno's Road before a row of houses, shortly branching right onto Pyllau Road. This soon becomes a dirt track and leads to the copper mines which you skirt around, keeping them to your right all the way.

Opposite the mine exit, turn left onto a grassy path to shortcut to the main summit road. Join this or stay on the verge to its left, then follow good paths towards the summit car park. Turn left just before the entrance and follow the wall downhill with grand views over Eryri.

On reaching the bottom corner of the wall, turn right and follow a good track parallel to it. This leads to a wonderful viewpoint at an ancient cairn at the far end of the wall. Continue to follow the wall around or trace the top of the small ridge to your left.

At the next corner, stay with the wall, merging with a gravel track, and keep ahead again until this breaks right away from the wall, where you will see St Tudno's and the cemetery below you to your left. Break left onto a grassy track and then turn left to follow a steep path down through the bracken to rejoin the road by the church. Turn left to finish.

Index

Aber Falls	90	Llandudno	94
Aberdaron	76	Llanrhychwyn	42
Aberglaslyn	24, 30	Llithfaen	78
Abergwyngregyn	90	Llynnau Cregennen	66
Abergynolwyn	70	Llyn Barfog (Bearded Lake)	72
Afon Conwy	46, 48	Llyn Crafnant	40
Afon Crafnant	42	Llyn Cwellyn	18
Afon Dwyfor	82	Llyn Cynwch	64
Afon Mawddach	60	Llyn Dinas	24
Afon y Cwm	26	Llyn Elsi	48
Barmouth	62	Llyn Geirionydd	40
Bearded Lake (Llyn Barfog)	72	Llyn Gwynant	28
Beddgelert	24, 30	Llyn Hafod-y-llyn	54
Beddgelert Forest	16, 22	Llyn Llywelyn	16, 22
Betws-y-Coed	46, 48	Llyn Mair	54
Bwlch y Moch	20	Llyn Padarn	12
Cadair Idris	68	Llyn Tecwyn Uchaf	56
Capel Curig	36, 38	Moel Siabod	36
Cefn Du	10	Nantmor	24, 30
Cnicht	32	Nant Gwernol	70
Coed Felenrhyd	56	Newborough Forest	84
Coed Ganllwyd	58	Pen y Cil	76
Coed y Brenin	60	Pen y Pass	20
Conwy Mountain	92	Plas y Brenin	38
Craflwyn	26	Pont Dyffrydan	68
Crib Goch	20	Pont Garreg-Hylldrem	52
Criccieth	82	Porth Swtan	88
Croesor	32, 52	Rhaeadr Ddu	58
Cwm Bychan	24	Rhyd Ddu	16, 18
Cwm Idwal	14	Snowdon (Yr Wyddfa)	18, 20
Cwm Penamnen	44	Traeth Llanddwyn	84
Dolgellau	64	Trefor	80
Dolwyddelan	44	Trefriw	42
Great Orme	94	Tre'r Ceiri hillfort	78
Gwydir Forest	40	Trwyn-y-Tâl	80
Holyhead Mountain	86	Yr Eifl	78
Llanberis	12	Yr Wyddfa (Snowdon)	18, 20